Get It Together for College

Get It Together for College

A Planner to Help You Get Organized and Get In

UPDATED
4th Edition

The College Board, New York, NY

About the College Board

The College Board is a mission-driven not-for-profit organization that connects students to college success and opportunity. Founded in 1900, the College Board was created to expand access to higher education. Today, the membership association is made up of over 6,000 of the world's leading educational institutions and is dedicated to promoting excellence and equity in education. Each year, the College Board helps more than seven million students prepare for a successful transition to college through programs and services in college readiness and college success—including the SAT® and the Advanced Placement Program®. The organization also serves the education community through research and advocacy on behalf of students, educators and schools. For further information, visit collegeboard.org.

Copies of this book are available from your local bookseller or may be ordered from College Board Publications, P.O. Box 7500, London, KY 40742-7500, or online through the College Board Store at www.collegeboard.org. The price is $15.99.

Editorial inquiries concerning this book should be directed to The College Board, 250 Vesey Street, New York, New York 10281.

ISBN: 978-1-4573-0926-7

Printed in the United States of America.

Distributed by Macmillan. For information on bulk purchases, please contact Macmillan Corporate and Premium Sales Department at (800) 221-7945, x5442.

Contents

Preface

You might be thinking the last thing you need right now is a book to read—that's just another brick on the pile. But this book is different. It doesn't add to the pile; it helps you manage the pile.

It does that by putting everything you need to know and remember in one handy, easy-to-find place. And, it makes it simple. No long articles to read, just quick tips, timelines, checklists, and places to keep track of things.

Much of the content in this book comes from the College Board website, collegeboard.org. Literally millions of high school students come to that site every year; chances are you are one of them. But often, a book is just handier and quicker than an app or website.

Like most big jobs, the college application process is really just a lot of little jobs spread out over a long period of time. The trick, of course, is to stay organized so you're not juggling these tasks blindfolded. If organizing a big project is not your strength, or you just have no experience at it, this book will help you.

Use it to keep the stress out, and to get in.

Acknowledgments

This book is a compilation of the expertise and sage advice of many people. Everyone involved with creating and maintaining the content on the #1 college website, collegeboard.org, should be credited here, but there just isn't enough space, so I hope a general shout-out will do. Thanks also to the people who helped publish this fourth edition: Jim Gwyn, Jennifer Rose, Tim Burke, and the production team at DataStream Content Solutions.

Some of the content in this book is adapted from other works, by permission of the copyright owners: "What to Include in a Sports Résumé" (page 45), adapted from material provided by Libertyville High School, Illinois; "Sample Student-Athlete Résumé" (page 46), adapted from material provided by Plano High School, Texas; and "Recommendation Cheat Sheet" on page 134, adapted from material provided by Lick-Wilmerding High School, California.

Tom Vanderberg
Senior Editor, Guidance Publications
The College Board

How to Use this Book

First of all, don't read this book all through, start to finish. It's not that kind of book. Just look up whatever you need to know about in the table of contents and go to a quick read about what to do or a handy tool to get it done.

But a few pointers are in order:

- The "Big Calendar" (Chapter 1) is the place to start, and to come back to for the big picture.
- There are separate timelines and "trackers" (to write down deadlines, etc.) for college admission applications, financial aid applications, scholarship applications, and the tests you might have to take.
- In case you miss them, there's a "College Fair Journal" in Chapter 4, and a "Campus Visit Journal" in Chapter 5; both can be handy to bring with you to write down your impressions.
- At the end of the book you'll find a place to write down the names, etc., of everyone you will meet and need to remember along the way.

Don't lose this book! It's going to make getting into college easier. And good luck!

My Organizer on collegeboard.org

Want to get organized online? Go to collegeboard.org's My Organizer to stay on top of college-planning milestones and make smart choices. Stay on track with deadline reminders and strategies that help you find, choose, get into, and afford the best college for you.

In My Organizer, you can:

- Get alerts, such as telling you the moment that your SAT® scores are released, or the next crucial step in your college planning.

- Get a big-picture view of what to do, and when, throughout each high school year to get ready for college.

- See upcoming dates and deadlines for tests, your college applications, and your favorite college's deadlines.

- See your PSAT/NMSQT® and SAT status and reminders.

- Use financial aid tools and calculators to search for scholarships, estimate college costs, calculate how college loans add up over time, and more.

- Watch videos of college students telling their own stories and educators sharing advice.

Chapter 1

The Big Calendar

The Summer Before

✔ **Read** interesting books—no matter what you go to college for, you'll need a good vocabulary and strong reading comprehension skills. Reading is also one of the best ways to prep for college entrance exams.

✔ **Get a social security number** if you don't already have one— you'll need it for your college applications.

✔ **Think about yourself.** What are your goals? What are you curious about? What are you good at? Knowing the basics about yourself will help you make the right college choices.

✔ **Talk to your family and friends** about college and your goals. They know you best and will have good insights.

NOTES

_____

_____

_____

_____

_____

September

✓ **Meet with your school counselor** to make sure you are taking the courses that colleges look for.

✓ **Resolve to get the best grades** you can this year. The payoff will be more colleges to choose from, and a better chance for scholarship money.

✓ **Pick up the** *PSAT/NMSQT Student Guide*® from your guidance office and take the practice test. (You'll take the real test in October.)

✓ Get involved in an **extracurricular activity**.

✓ Find out if your school will have a **college night**.

NOTES

October

✔ Take the **PSAT/NMSQT**.

✔ Attend a **college fair**.

✔ Begin looking through college guidebooks and websites—
start a preliminary list of colleges that might interest you.

✔ Start to **learn about financial aid**. Attend a family financial
aid night at your school or in your area, and use the Net Price
Calculator at collegeboard.org to estimate how much aid you
might receive.

NOTES

_____

_____

_____

_____

_____

November

✔ Begin to **research scholarships**—use the Scholarship Search on collegeboard.org to find out about deadlines and eligibility requirements.

✔ **Learn about the SAT®.** Go to sat.org. Also, pick up the official bulletins at your guidance office.

✔ If you are planning to major in the arts (drama, music, fine art), ask your teachers about requirements for a **portfolio or audition**.

NOTES

December

✔ Review your **PSAT/NMSQT Score Report** with your school counselor. Talk about what courses to take next year, based on your results.

✔ Spend time over the holidays to **think about what kind of college** you want. Big or small? Far away or close to home?

✔ **Make a list** of the college features that are important to you.

✔ **Begin preparing for the SAT.** Visit the free SAT prep section at satpractice.org.

NOTES

_____

_____

_____

_____

_____

January

✔ **Meet with your school counselor** to talk about the colleges you are interested in, what entrance exams you should take, and when you should take them.

✔ If English is not your primary language, decide when to take the **TOEFL** test.

✔ Start thinking about **what you want to study in college**. Use resources like the majors and careers section at collegeboard.org.

✔ **Register for the SAT** if you want to take it in **March**.

NOTES

February

✓ Think about which teachers you will ask to write **letters of recommendation**.

✓ If you're in Advanced Placement Program® (AP®) classes, **register for AP Exams**, given in May.

✓ Ask your counselor or teacher about taking the **SAT Subject Tests**™ in the spring. You should take them while course material is still fresh in your mind.

NOTES

_____

_____

_____

_____

_____

March

✔ **Register for the SAT and/or SAT Subject Tests** if you want to take them in **May**.

✔ **Narrow your college list** to a reasonable number. Explore the college's websites, read their brochures and catalogs, and talk to your family and friends.

✔ **Practice the SAT**. Ask your school counselor for the *SAT Student Guide*—it's free and has a full-length practice test; you can also download free tests from satpractice.org.

NOTES

_____

_____

_____

_____

_____

April

✓ **Register for the SAT and/or SAT Subject Tests** if you want to take them in **June**.

✓ **Plan your courses for senior year.** Make sure you are going to meet the high school course requirements for your top-choice colleges.

✓ **Plan campus visits.** It's best to go when classes are in session. Start with colleges that are close by.

NOTES

_____

_____

_____

_____

_____

May

✓ **Register for the SAT and/or SAT Subject Tests** if you want to take them in **August**.

✓ Talk to your coach and your counselor about **NCAA requirements** if you want to play Division I or II sports in college.

✓ Start looking for a **summer job or volunteer work**—the good ones go fast.

✓ **AP Exams** are given.

NOTES

June

✔ Ask your counselor about **local scholarships** offered by church groups, civic associations, and businesses in your community.

✔ If you are considering **military academies or ROTC** scholarships, contact your counselor before leaving school for the summer.

NOTES

_____

_____

_____

_____

_____

The Summer Before

✓ **Register for the SAT and/or SAT Subject Tests** if you want to take them in **October or November**.

✓ If you want to play a NCAA Division I or II sport in college, **register with the NCAA Eligibility Center** (**www.ncaa.org**).

✓ **Visit colleges** on your list. Call ahead for the campus tour schedule.

✓ Begin working on your **college application essays**.

✓ **Write a résumé** (accomplishments, activities, and work experiences) to help you later with your college applications.

✓ If you are applying to a **visual or performing arts program**, work on your portfolio or audition pieces.

NOTES

September

✓ Meet with your school counselor to **finalize your list of colleges**. Be sure your list includes "safety," "reach," and "probable" schools.

✓ **Get an FSA ID** for both yourself and one of your parents from **www.fafsa.ed.gov**. You'll need them to submit the FAFSA financial aid form, which you can submit any time after October 1.

✓ If you can't afford application fees, your counselor can help you request a **fee waiver**.

✓ Set up **campus visits and interviews**; attend open houses at colleges that interest you.

✓ Find out if there will be a **family financial aid night** at your school, or elsewhere nearby, and put it on your calendar.

NOTES

October

✓ **Register for the SAT and/or SAT Subject Tests** if you want to take them in **December or January**.

✓ **Start working on your FAFSA** and submit it as soon as you can. Go to **www.fafsa.ed.gov** to access the form.

✓ If you are going to apply under an **Early Decision or Early Action** plan, get started now. Some colleges have October deadlines.

✓ **Ask for letters of recommendation** from your counselor, teachers, coaches, or employers.

✓ Write **first drafts of your college essays** and ask your parents and teachers to review them.

✓ If you need to fill out the **CSS Profile™**, you can register on collegeboard.org starting Oct. 1.

NOTES

November

✔ **Finish your application essays**. Proofread them rigorously for mistakes.

✔ **Apply to colleges with rolling admission** (first-come, first-served) as early as possible. Keep hard copies.

✔ Make sure your **test scores** will be sent by the testing agency to each one of your colleges.

✔ Give your school counselor the proper **forms to send transcripts** to your colleges in plenty of time to meet deadlines.

NOTES

_____

_____

_____

_____

_____

December

✔ Try to **wrap up college applications** before winter break. Make copies for yourself and your school counselor.

✔ If you applied for **Early Decision**, you should have an answer by Dec. 15. If you are denied or deferred, submit applications now to other colleges.

✔ **Apply for scholarships** in time to meet application deadlines.

✔ **Contact the financial aid office** at the colleges on your list to see if they require any **other financial aid forms**.

NOTES
_____
_____
_____
_____
_____

January

✓ **Submit your FAFSA** if you haven't already! Check your college's financial aid deadlines and priority dates; some can be as early as Feb. 1.

✓ **Submit other financial aid forms** that may be required—such as the CSS Profile or the college's own forms. Keep copies.

✓ If a college wants to see your **midyear grades**, give the form to your school counselor.

✓ If you have any **new honors or accomplishments** that were not in your original application, let your colleges know.

NOTES

February

✔ **Contact your colleges** to confirm that all application materials have been received.

✔ If need be, correct or update your **Student Aid Report (SAR)** that follows the FAFSA.

✔ If any **special circumstances** affect your family's financial situation, alert each college's financial aid office.

✔ **File income tax returns early**. Some colleges want more current tax information before finalizing financial aid offers.

✔ Make sure you're registered for **AP Exams** you want to take. (If you are home schooled or your school does not offer AP, you must contact AP Services by March 1.)

NOTES

March

✔ **Admission decisions start arriving**. Read everything you receive carefully, as some may require prompt action on your part.

✔ **Revisit colleges** that accepted you if it's hard to make a choice.

✔ Send copies of your **FAFSA to any scholarship programs** that require it as part of their applications.

✔ **Don't get senioritis!** Colleges want to see strong second half grades.

NOTES

_____

_____

_____

_____

_____

April

✓ **Carefully compare financial aid award letters** from the colleges that accept you—it might not be clear which is the better offer. If you have questions, contact the college's financial aid office or talk to your school counselor.

✓ **If you don't get enough aid**, consider your options, which include appealing the award.

✓ Make a final decision, **accept the aid package and mail a deposit check** to the college you select before May 1 (the acceptance deadline for most schools).

✓ **Notify the other colleges** that you won't be attending (so another student can have your spot).

NOTES

_____

_____

_____

_____

_____

May

✔ AP Exams are given. Make sure your **AP Grade Report** is sent to your college.

✔ **Study hard for final exams**. Most offers of admission are contingent on your final grades.

✔ **Thank everyone** who wrote you recommendations or otherwise helped with your college applications.

✔ **If you weren't accepted** anywhere, don't give up—you still have options. Talk to your school counselor about them.

NOTES

_____

_____

_____

_____

_____

June

✓ Have your counselor send your **final transcript** to your college choice.

✓ If you plan on competing in Division I or Division II college sports, have your counselor send your final transcript to the **NCAA Eligibility Center**.

✓ Think about your **summer job options**. The more money you make, the easier it will be to finance college—and have some fun during the school year.

✓ Enjoy your graduation, and have a great summer!

NOTES

_____

_____

_____

_____

_____

Make Sure You're on Track

What Colleges Are Looking For

As you get ready to apply to colleges, be sure you know what counts most in the minds of college admission officers. Here's a quick rundown.

Most important: your high school transcript

This is what colleges will look at first and foremost. The grades you earned in high school are the best predictor of college success. Your transcript also shows whether you've taken the required or recommended college-prep courses.

But colleges won't just look at your grades and which courses you took—they will also look at how challenging those courses were. So a hard-fought-for C+ in AP Biology might outweigh an easy A in an introductory computer class.

> "The first thing most colleges and universities will consider will be the high school courses a student chose. Are they challenging? Are they college prep, honors, or AP courses?"
>
> — Mary Ellen Anderson, director of admissions, Indiana University–Bloomington

Test scores are just part of the picture

Your scores on college entrance exams are only one of a number of factors that colleges will consider. Most often, admission officers will use your test scores to supplement your high school transcript or help them interpret it. That's because high schools across the country can vary greatly in terms of grading standards and course rigor, and standardized tests offer a way to compare your application with others on a level playing field.

Beyond the numbers

Very few colleges assess applications using just transcripts and test scores. Other factors, like essays, recommendations, interviews, and extracurricular activities, also play a role in admission decisions.

All of these additional factors help admission officers look "beyond the numbers" and see what kind of person you really are. None of these factors will be the most important thing the college looks at; but taken together they can help round out your application and tip the scale in your favor.

Here's a closer look at each of the personal factors colleges usually look at:

Recommendations give the college a sense of your overall attitude toward learning, your character, and the context for the grades on your transcript. For tips on choosing whom to ask for recommendations, and how to ask them, see page 132.

Your record of extracurricular activities, in and out of school, tells the college about how involved you are in your school and local community. From that, they'll have a good picture of how likely you are to contribute to their own campus community. For tips on choosing extra-curriculars, see page 34.

Essays are the one component over which you have total control. For tips on writing your essays, see Chapter 8.

Interviews are rarely required and don't carry a great deal of weight in the overall application. Think of them as an opportunity to put a personal face on your application, and to learn more about whether the college would be a good fit for you. You'll find more about interviews, including checklists of questions to expect and questions you should ask, in Chapter 9.

> "If students try to force themselves to look like a fit to the admissions committee, that's like putting square pegs in round holes—they will be unhappy."
>
> — Deren Finks, former dean of admission and financial aid, Harvey Mudd College

How interested are you?

Competitive colleges weigh an additional factor: "demonstrated interest." That means they try to determine whether, if they accept you, you will actually enroll at their college.

Here are some things that colleges usually look for when they try to gauge your level of interest:

- Did you contact the college for information about their programs?
- Have you talked to anyone from the college at a college fair or on a campus visit?
- If you interviewed with the college, did you ask in-depth questions that show you've already researched the college?

Always keep in mind:

The most important thing is what *you* want and what *you* are looking for. You're not selling, you're buying, even if it's a "reach" school.

Ninth- and Tenth-Grade Planner

If you're a ninth- or tenth-grader and have this book in your hand, good for you! You're thinking about college while there is still time to plan ahead. Here's some important groundwork that should take place in your first two years of high school.

Grade 9

Meet with your school counselor

Find out what high school courses colleges want to see on your transcript (see the chart to the right), and make sure your ninth-grade courses are on the right track.

With your counselor, map out what courses should be taken during the rest of high school.

Get involved in an extracurricular activity

Get into something you will really enjoy doing, even if it's not that popular. (See "Extracurricular Tips" on page 34.)

If you want to play a sport in college, talk to your coach about eligibility requirements (see "Tips for the Student-Athlete" on page 44).

Start thinking about careers

Having a career goal will help you stay focused in high school. You might change your mind a lot, but it's the thought process that counts.

Save for college

It's still not too late to start a college savings plan. Every little bit helps! Talk about college costs and financial aid options with your parents.

Grade 10

Meet with your school counselor—again

Make sure you are enrolled in the right college-prep courses and on the right track for junior and senior year.

If your school offers the PSAT 10, take it

It's a good idea to take the PSAT 10 because it provides invaluable feedback that will show what you're doing well, and what you should work on while there is still ample time to improve.

Are you interested in attending a U.S. military academy?

If so, you should request a precandidate questionnaire and complete it. Your school counselor can help you with that.

Tour a college campus in your area

Even if you are not interested in attending the college you are visiting, it will help you learn what to look for in a college.

If you don't have a social security number, apply for one

You'll need it for college applications, testing, scholarships, and other opportunities.

Recommended High School Classes

Here are the most commonly recommended classes. They're geared for students headed to a four-year college, but you should take most of them if you're also interested in a two-year college.

What colleges want you to take in high school

SUBJECT	CLASSES	
ENGLISH/LANGUAGE ARTS (8 credits/4 years)	literature writing/composition speech/rhetoric	
MATH (6 credits/3 years*)	algebra I algebra II geometry trigonometry and/or calculus	
SCIENCE (WITH LAB) (6 credits/3 years*)	biology chemistry and/or physics earth/space sciences	
SOCIAL STUDIES (6 credits/3 years*)	U.S. history U.S. government world history or geography	
FOREIGN LANGUAGE (4 credits/2 years)	*More selective colleges will require 3 to 4 years.*	
VISUAL/PERFORMING ARTS (1 to 2 credits)	*Choose from:* studio art dance	music drama
OTHER (1 to 2 credits)	*Choose from:* business computer science/applications environmental studies/science government and politics	communications economics statistics

* More competitive colleges will want to see four years each of math, lab science, and social studies.

High School Planning Worksheet

Fill out a worksheet for each year of school, listing the courses that you've taken, are currently taking, or plan to take. Talk to your counselor about your plan and make sure you're on track to meet college requirements.

SUBJECT	9TH GRADE		10TH GRADE	
	FALL SEMESTER	SPRING SEMESTER	FALL SEMESTER	SPRING SEMESTER
ENGLISH/ LANGUAGE ARTS				
HISTORY/ SOCIAL STUDIES				
MATH				
SCIENCE (INDICATE IF LAB)				
FOREIGN LANGUAGE				
ARTS				
OTHER				

	11TH GRADE		12TH GRADE	
FALL SEMESTER	SPRING SEMESTER	FALL SEMESTER	SPRING SEMESTER	

10 Questions to Ask Your School Counselor

Your school counselor is your best resource as you plan for college, and will be your partner in getting your college applications completed. If it's hard to get face time with your counselor, use e-mail to get a conversation started with these basic questions:

1. What courses do I need to take to be ready for college?

2. Which elective courses do you recommend?

3. What AP courses are available, and how do I get in?

4. Do you have any college planning sessions scheduled?

5. What should I be doing at home and over the summer to get ready for college?

6. What kinds of grades do different colleges require?

7. Are there any college fairs at this school, or nearby?

8. Where do other kids from this school attend college?

9. Do you have any information to help me start exploring careers?

10. Are there any local scholarships or awards that I should know about now, so I can work toward them?

What to Know About AP®

Advanced Placement Program (AP) courses are designed to give high school students the chance to study a subject at the level of an introductory college course. AP Exams are offered in May for all AP subjects (except Studio Art, which is scored on the basis of a portfolio). Depending upon your exam score and on the AP policy at the college you attend, you may be eligible for college credit for that course and/or advanced placement into a higher-level college course.

The difference between credit and placement

Some colleges award credit for qualifying AP Exam scores. This means that you actually earn points toward your college degree. Others award advanced placement. This means that when you're in college, you can skip introductory courses, enter higher-level classes, and/or fulfill general education requirements.

The benefits of earning college credit or placement

College credit or placement can allow you to move into upper-level courses sooner, pursue a double major or a combined bachelor's/master's degree program, gain time to study and travel abroad, and complete your undergraduate degree in fewer than four years.

Why you need to take the AP Exam in order to earn college credit or placement

Colleges and universities give credit or placement only for qualifying AP Exam scores, not AP course grades. Without a corresponding AP Exam score, they can't verify how well you've mastered college-level content.

> Through AP, you can earn college credit worth hundreds of dollars— even thousands at some colleges.

What else you can get out of AP

There's more to AP than the possibility of earning college credit or placement. You might even consider these additional benefits to be more important. By taking an AP course, you can:

- Study subjects in greater depth and detail
- Exercise your writing skills, reasoning ability, and problem-solving techniques
- Develop the study habits necessary for tackling rigorous course work
- Show colleges your willingness to challenge yourself

How to get started

Talk to an AP teacher or the AP Coordinator at your school about the course you want to take. Discuss the course's workload and any preparation you might need. If you are homeschooled or attend a school that doesn't offer AP, you can still participate through independent study or by taking online AP courses.

Extracurricular Tips

Selective colleges want to know what you do both inside and outside the classroom. Yes, your academics come first, but what you do with your free time reveals a lot, such as:

- Whether you are mature enough to stick to something over the long haul
- What your nonacademic interests are—what makes you tick
- How you've contributed to something beyond yourself
- Whether you can manage your time and priorities

So here are some tips for choosing extracurriculars.

Consider your interests and abilities first

It's easier to commit to something that fits the real you. While it's natural to want to be where your friends are, don't join something for that reason alone—it truly should be a shared interest.

Go for depth, not breadth

Don't join a bunch of activities just to bulk up your application. Colleges are more impressed by a real commitment to one activity over time, rather than a superficial involvement in multiple activities.

Keep your balance

Remember: Colleges are not interested in seeing you "do it all." Don't overextend and risk burnout or bad grades. Colleges don't have a checklist of requirements when it comes to extracurriculars.

You don't have to be a star

Don't worry about being president of the club, or captain of the team. The key is whether you've contributed something significant—center stage or behind the scenes.

If you're not a joiner

Selective colleges aren't looking for extracurricular activities to see how well you play with others; they're looking for evidence of your nonacademic qualities and experience. Good news: You can show that even if you don't like to join teams or clubs. As school counselor Dorothy Coppock puts it: "An avid equestrian or ice-skater does not need to add on a school activity to look well-rounded."

Working or volunteering counts too

A job—paid or unpaid—shows that you can handle responsibilities and have "real-world" experience. If jobs are hard to find, ask your counselor how to arrange for an internship or a job-shadowing opportunity. The local chamber of commerce or organizations like Rotary or Kiwanis might also be able to help you.

Volunteer work, such as tutoring elementary school kids or spending time at a local hospital, is another great way to gain the skills and experience colleges like to see. Opportunities to help out are easy to find in every community.

Extracurricular Archive

Keep a record of all your activities as you go through high school. It will be good to have on hand when it's time to fill out college applications or if you need to provide a student résumé.

9TH GRADE   School activities: *[e.g., sports, clubs, special projects]*

School awards: *[e.g., honor roll]*

Community activities: *[e.g., food drive, church choir, beach clean-up day]*

Work experience: *[include hours/week]*

10TH GRADE   School activities:

School awards:

Community activities:

Work experience:

11TH GRADE   School activities:

School awards:

Community activities:

Work experience:

12TH GRADE   School activities:

School awards:

Community activities:

Work experience:

Top 10 Time-Management Tips

Does it seem like there's never enough time in the day to get everything done? Feel like you're always running late? Here are the top 10 tips for taking control of your life. Remember, the easiest way to break bad habits is to focus on making new habits.

1. Make a "to do" list every day

Put things that are most important at the top and do them first. If it's easier, use a planner to track all of your tasks. And don't forget to reward yourself for your accomplishments.

2. Use spare minutes wisely

Get some reading done on the bus ride home from school, for example, and you'll kill two birds with one stone.

3. It's okay to say "no"

If you're asked to babysit on a Thursday night and you have a final exam the next day, realize that it's okay to say no. Keep your short- and long-term priorities in mind.

4. Find the right time

You'll work more efficiently if you figure out when you do your best work. For example, if your brain handles math better in the afternoon, don't wait to do it until late at night.

5. Review your notes every day

You'll reinforce what you've learned, so you need less time to study. You'll also be ready if your teacher calls on you or gives a pop quiz.

6. Get a good night's sleep

Running on empty makes the day seem longer and your tasks seem more difficult.

7. Let your friends know

If texting, Facebook, phone calls, etc., are too tempting and distracting during homework and study time, tell your friends (and yourself) that you are offline and unavailable between 8 and 10 p.m. (or whenever). Blame your folks if you must.

8. Become a taskmaster

Figure out how much free time you have each week. Give yourself a time budget and plan your activities accordingly. (Use the "Personal Time-Making Machine" on the next page.)

9. Don't waste time agonizing

Have you ever wasted an entire evening by worrying about something that you're supposed to be doing? Was it worth it? Instead of agonizing and procrastinating, just do it.

10. Keep things in perspective

Setting goals that are unrealistic sets you up for failure. While it's good to set high goals for yourself, be sure not to overdo it. Good goals are both challenging and reachable.

Your Personal Time-Making Machine

Want to create more time to get things done? Use this worksheet to see what you do in a normal school week (a seven-day week = 168 hours), and figure out where you can make more time.

HOW MANY HOURS A DAY DO YOU SPEND:	DAILY TOTAL	FREQUENCY	WEEKLY TOTAL
Sleeping (yes, include naps)?		× 7 =	
In school?		× 5 =	
Studying or doing homework?		× 7 =	
On extracurricular activities and sports?		× 7 =	
Watching TV, playing video games, or relaxing?		× 7 =	
Online or on the computer?		× 7 =	
Texting or talking on the phone?		× 7 =	
Hanging out?		× 7 =	
Working at a job?		× 7 =	
Traveling to and from school, work, lessons, etc.?		× 7 =	
On meals (preparing, eating, and cleaning up)?		× 7 =	
Taking showers, getting dressed, etc.?		× 7 =	
Doing chores?		× 7 =	
Other stuff (list):		× 7 =	

TOTAL HOURS

EXTRA TIME AVAILABLE (168 hours minus your total)

Summer Reading List

Reading is essential college prep but it doesn't have to be a chore. Pick books you'll enjoy reading by googling the title for a quick synopsis or review.

This list was compiled from several lists recommended by high schools, libraries, and other organizations, but it's geared toward more contemporary, less typical suggestions.

Fiction

AUTHOR	TITLE	DATE
Alemanndine, Rabih	*The Hakawati*	2008
Allende, Isabel	*Portrait in Sepia*	2000
Allison, Dorothy	*Bastard Out of Carolina*	1992
Alvarez, Julia	*In the Time of Butterflies*	1994
Atwood, Margaret	*Oryx and Crake*	2003
Brooks, Geraldine	*March*	2005
Card, Orson Scott	*Ender's Game*	1985
Cisneros, Sandra	*The House on Mango Street*	1991
Crutcher, Chris	*Deadline*	2007
Danticat, Edwidge	*The Farming of Bones*	1998
Denfeld, Rene	*The Enchanted*	2014
Erdrich, Louise	*The Plague of Doves*	2009
Fowler, Karen Joy	*We Are All Completely Beside Ourselves*	2014
Gaines, Ernest	*A Lesson Before Dying*	1993
Greenberg, Joanne	*In This Sign*	1970
Guterson, David	*Snow Falling On Cedars*	1994
Haruf, Kent	*Plainsong*	1999
Holthe, Tess Uriza	*When the Elephants Dance*	2002
Hosseini, Khaled	*A Thousand Splendid Suns*	2007
Ishiguro, Kazuo	*Never Let Me Go*	2005
Johnson, James Weldon	*Autobiography of an Ex-Colored Man*	1991
Klass, David	*Home of the Braves*	2002
Klay, Phil	*Redeployment*	2014
Lahiri, Jhumpa	*The Lowland*	2013
Lamb, Wally	*She's Come Undone*	1992
Leckie, Ann	*Ancillary Justice*	2013
Lightman, Alan	*The Diagnosis*	2000
Marlantes, Karl	*Matterhorn: A Novel of the Vietnam War*	2010
Mason, Bobbie Ann	*In Country*	1985
Miller, Walter M. Jr.	*A Canticle for Leibowitz*	1964
Mitchell, David	*Black Swan Green*	2006
Mori, Kyoko	*Shizuko's Daughter*	1993
Morrison, Toni	*Jazz*	1992
Naidoo, Beverly	*The Other Side of Truth*	2001

AUTHOR	TITLE	DATE
Obreht, Téa	*The Tiger's Wife*	2011
Ozeki, Ruth	*A Tale for the Time Being*	2013
Power, Susan	*The Grass Dancer*	1994
Proulx, Annie E.	*The Shipping News*	1993
Price, Richard	*Lush Life*	2008
Robinson, Marilynne	*Lila*	2014
Shaara, Michael	*Killer Angels*	1974
Smiley, Jane	*A Thousand Acres*	1993
Spiegelman, Art	*Maus: A Survivor's Tale*	1986
Stoker, Bram	*Dracula*	1897
Tsukiyama, Gail	*The Samurai's Garden*	1996
Uchida, Yoshiko	*Picture Bride*	1987
Walker, Margaret	*Jubilee*	1967
Ward, Jesmyn	*Salvage the Bones*	2012
Wolff, Tobias	*Old School*	2003
Woodrell, Daniel	*Winter's Bone*	2006
Yolen, Jane	*Briar Rose*	1992

Nonfiction

AUTHOR	TITLE	DATE
Ackerman, Diane	*The Human Age*	2014
Anders, Lars	*The Storm and the Tide*	2014
Branch, John	*Boys on Ice: The Life and Death of Derek Boogaard*	2014
Codell, Esmé Raji	*Educating Esmé: Diary of a Teacher's First Year*	2009
Ehrenreich, Barbara	*Nickel and Dimed: On (Not) Getting By in America*	2001
Eire, Carlos	*Waiting for Snow in Havana: Confessions of a Cuban Boy*	2003
Fink, Sheri	*Five Days at Memorial*	2013
Finkel, David	*Thank You for Your Service*	2013
Gopal, Anand	*No Good Men Among the Living*	2014
Gore, Al	*An Inconvenient Truth*	2006
Gordon, Kim	*Girl in a Band*	2015
Hawking, Stephen	*A Briefer History of Time*	2005
Hillenbrand, Lauren	*Unbroken*	2010
Keegan, Maria	*The Opposite of Loneliness*	2014
Keneally, Thomas	*Schindler's List*	1982
Krakauer, Jon	*Into Thin Air*	1997
Larson, Erik	*Dead Wake*	2015
McCall, Nathan	*Makes Me Wanna Holler: A Young Black Man in America*	1975
McCourt, Frank	*Angela's Ashes*	1996
Miller, Ethelbert	*Fathering Words: The Making of an African American Writer*	2000
Munroe, Randall	*What If?*	2014
Sides, Hampton	*In the Kingdom of Ice*	2014
Urrea, Luis Alberto	*The Devil's Highway: A True Story*	2004
Wiesel, Elie	*Night*	1972
Yiwu, Liao	*For a Song and a Hundred Songs*	2013

NOTES

If You Want to Play Sports

Tips for the Student-Athlete

Do you feel that you have what it takes to play sports at the college level? Then you need to do some work "off the field" to get yourself noticed and recruited by college coaches. Here are some tips on what you need to do.

Talk with your coach

First, have an honest talk about your athletic ability. Your coach can give you a realistic appraisal of your chances, and make some suggestions about which college athletic programs you can aspire to.

Find out about academic eligibility rules

These rules are set down by the various athletic associations. In order to be considered by an NCAA Division I school, for example, you must achieve a minimum GPA in 16 core courses in high school, and achieve a minimum combined score on either the SAT or ACT.

Attend a sports camp

Gain an edge over the summer vacation.

Start a sports résumé

And keep it updated. The purpose of the résumé is to give coaches a quick idea of who you are, what you've done, what your athletic potential may be, and whether you are academically eligible to be recruited.

Send letters of interest to coaches

Send them to the coach at each college you are interested in. (See "Sample Student-Athlete Letter of Interest" on page 47.) Get the name of the coach from the college's website. Try to send the letters as early in your junior year as possible. If the college has a prospect questionnaire on its website, complete that too.

Register with the NCAA eligibility center

Register at the end of your junior year. You won't be eligible to play NCAA Division I or II sports or receive an athletic scholarship otherwise. It's easy and you can do it online. Read the current NCAA *Guide for the College-Bound Student-Athlete* available at ncaapublications.com.

Make a performance or skills video

Ask your coach for advice on how to do this before the season starts. Editing is key: It has to be short (no longer than 5 minutes) or college coaches won't watch it.

Follow up

If you receive profile forms or questionnaires from coaches, complete and return them as soon as possible. Follow up with a telephone call from you, not your parents.

As you look at colleges, see the big picture

Don't focus on their sports programs only. It's really important that the college you end up at is a good fit for you both academically and personally, so that you will be happy there even if you don't end up playing a sport. It's also important to have realistic expectations about athletic scholarships—they are hard to come by and easy to lose, so look at the financial aid opportunities at each college as well.

What to Include in a Sports Résumé

As you can see from the sample résumé on the next page, your sports résumé should include your academic stats as well as athletic.

If you can, include your time for sprints and longer distances. No matter what sport you play, how fast you can move (and for how long) is important info.

It also helps if you can give information that would shed light on the caliber of your competition, such as a ranking, or whether you competed in county or state finals.

Statistics to include in a résumé, listed by sport

BASEBALL AND SOFTBALL
Batting average
Fielding percentage
Earned run average, or ERA
   (pitchers)
Win–loss record (pitchers)
Runs batted in (RBI)
Stolen bases

BASKETBALL
Assists (per game)
Rebounds
Free-throw percentage
Field-goal percentage (2 point and
   3 point)
Blocked shots

CROSS-COUNTRY, TRACK AND FIELD
Distance in field events: shot put,
   discus, long jump, triple jump
Height in field events: high jump
   and pole vault
Time and distance
Conference, invitational, or state
   places

FIELD HOCKEY
Goals
Assists
Blocked shots

FOOTBALL
Tackles (defensive player)
Assists (defensive player)
Sacks (defensive player)
Interceptions (defensive/back/
   linebacker)
Fumbles recovered
Yards rushing (running back)
Receptions—yards, average,
   touchdowns
Attempts, completions, total yards
   passing/rushing (quarterback)
Punts—attempts, longest, average
Kickoff returns—attempts, longest,
   average
Points scored—touchdowns, extra
   points
Field goals—attempts, longest,
   average, total points scored

GOLF
Scores
Handicap

GYMNASTICS
Events and scores
Conference, invitational, or state
   places

SOCCER
Goals
Assists and blocked shots

SWIMMING
Event and times
Dives, difficulty, scores
Major conference, invitational, or
   state places

TENNIS
Record and ranking
Major conference, invitational, or
   state ranking

VOLLEYBALL
Blocks
Assists
Kills
Aces

WRESTLING
Individual record and at what weight
Season takedowns
Season reversals
Season escapes
Season 2-point and 3-point near fall
   points
Falls
Conference, invitational, or state
   places

Sample
Student-Athlete Résumé

John J. Anybody
123 Any Street
Anytown, TX 75075
555 234-5678
soccerplayer@fastmail.com

Academics:	Anytown Senior High School 2000 Crosstown Parkway Anytown, TX 75075 555-234-1000 Expected graduation: June 2019 Expected college major: Business	SAT Scores: Reading/Writing 510, Math 540 GPA: 3.2 (4.0 scale)
Personal Statistics:	Date of Birth: May 20, 2001 Height: 5′11″ Weight: 165 lbs.	40-yard time: 4.95 secs. 100-yard time: 10.9 secs. Mile time: 5.12 mins.
My Sport:	Soccer	

Athletic History:

- Soccer, freshman: left wing, junior varsity; 11 goals, 21 assists. Team finished second in league, 12–4.
- Soccer, sophomore: right wing, varsity; 9 goals, 24 assists. Team finished first in league; named Honorable Mention All-County.
- Soccer, junior: right wing, varsity; 23 goals, 19 assists. Team reached state quarter finals; named to third team All-State. Elected team captain for senior year.
- Track, sophomore: quarter mile, best time, 52.8.

References: John Pele, Varsity Soccer Coach, Anytown Senior High School
Arnold Johnson, Director, All-American Soccer Camp

Sample Student-Athlete Letter of Interest

You can send the same letter to the coaches at all the colleges you are interested in. Just be sure to double-check that the correct names of the colleges and coaches match up. Use snail-mail, not e-mail. Make a copy for your high school coach.

If the college has a prospect/recruit questionnaire on its website, fill that in too.

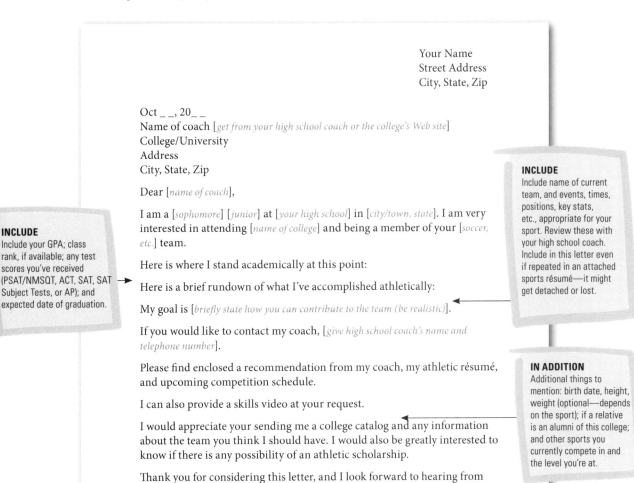

Your Name
Street Address
City, State, Zip

Oct _ _, 20_ _
Name of coach [*get from your high school coach or the college's Web site*]
College/University
Address
City, State, Zip

Dear [*name of coach*],

I am a [*sophomore*] [*junior*] at [*your high school*] in [*city/town, state*]. I am very interested in attending [*name of college*] and being a member of your [*soccer, etc.*] team.

Here is where I stand academically at this point:

Here is a brief rundown of what I've accomplished athletically:

My goal is [*briefly state how you can contribute to the team (be realistic)*].

If you would like to contact my coach, [*give high school coach's name and telephone number*].

Please find enclosed a recommendation from my coach, my athletic résumé, and upcoming competition schedule.

I can also provide a skills video at your request.

I would appreciate your sending me a college catalog and any information about the team you think I should have. I would also be greatly interested to know if there is any possibility of an athletic scholarship.

Thank you for considering this letter, and I look forward to hearing from you.

Sincerely,

INCLUDE
Include your GPA; class rank, if available; any test scores you've received (PSAT/NMSQT, ACT, SAT, SAT Subject Tests, or AP); and expected date of graduation.

INCLUDE
Include name of current team, and events, times, positions, key stats, etc., appropriate for your sport. Review these with your high school coach. Include in this letter even if repeated in an attached sports résumé—it might get detached or lost.

IN ADDITION
Additional things to mention: birth date, height, weight (optional—depends on the sport); if a relative is an alumni of this college; and other sports you currently compete in and the level you're at.

Finding Colleges
You Like

Quick Start
College Search Tips

Feeling overwhelmed by the whole idea of finding the perfect college out of the thousands of colleges in the United States? Don't be. Once you realize that there is no such thing as one perfect college for you, but rather a slew of colleges that would be a pretty good fit, you can begin to relax—and begin the search.

Here are some quick and easy things you can do today to start the process.

Decide on how near or far to look

Setting geographic parameters is the easiest way to cut your search down to size. Talk to your parents about the pros and cons of commuting from home or living away. Think about how often you would like to come home, what kind of environment you would like to live in, and what the realistic possibilities are.

Read what colleges send you

At this point, you're probably receiving tons of information about colleges by way of brochures, posts, and e-mails. Looking through this material will help you begin to learn about specific colleges—and it may also show you options you didn't know you had.

Talk to family and friends

Get the perspective of people who have already gone to college or are in college now. Their personal experiences can give you insight into what college is all about. Ask relatives about their alma mater or talk to older siblings and friends home for the holidays.

Write down what you want or need

Coed or single-sex? Public or private? Making a list of criteria will help you determine what's most important. (See the "What You Want Checklist" on page 78.) Use this list to make search queries in collegeboard.org's College Search so you can find schools that match. (But remember, too many queries in one search will usually result in no match found.)

Make a college wish list

List any college that looks good to you. At this point, don't limit yourself. Just brainstorm. Keep an open mind and try to look a little beyond your parameters as well—you might stumble across a college you never thought of that has something really exciting to offer. And it just might be the college nearby.

Don't worry about cost yet.

You won't know if a college is too expensive until you find out how much financial aid they offer you. It just might turn out that a really expensive school gives you enough aid to make it affordable.

Do a deeper dive

Check out the college's website to take a virtual tour, see the courses offered, and contact students and the admission office. Visit the college's Facebook page and follow it on Twitter (see "10 Tips for Using Social Media" on page 54).

Visit a nearby campus

Go to a college that's close to home or one that a friend or family member already attends. It doesn't even have to be one that you're interested in attending. Visiting will help you focus your preferences and may even make you think of needs you didn't know you had. Can't get to a campus? Take a virtual tour on the school's website.

Go to a college fair

Ask your school counselor if there's a college fair coming to your school or a nearby school. Once there, you can pick up catalogs, talk to representatives and other students, and feel like you're officially starting the search process. (See the "College Fair Tip Sheet" on page 71.)

Meet with your counselor

He or she is drawing on years of experience matching students to colleges that could be a good fit.

Don't get hung up on one school

If you think you must attend a "name-brand" college, or that there is only one perfect college out there for you, you might set yourself up for disappointment. Truth is, there are many colleges where you can be happy and get a great education. Aim for a list of several "first-choice" colleges.

10 Tips for Surfing College Websites

Not all college websites are created equal. Some are better designed than others; some are easier to navigate; and some are better at keeping information current. Use the site map if you have trouble finding any of the information described below.

1. Look for social media links

Most college websites link to social media on the campus network or on sites like Facebook and YouTube. Some college websites also provide mashups of all their updates on those sites. This provides a great way for you to see what the school is like through its online community.

You should never feel pressured to "friend" anyone in these communities—just take it as an open invitation to ask questions from either students or staff and as a way to find others with the same interests and questions about the school as you.

2. Lurk in the halls of student government

These legislative bodies can be key players on campus, controlling a wide range of student services. Online, you can get an idea of just how seriously they take their responsibilities. You may even be able to read the minutes of a recent meeting.

3. Go clubbing

Are you an activist? A demon at the chessboard? A future marketing exec? A tree-hugger? Clubs come in all shapes and sizes. Look for links like Student Life to find out if there are campus clubs you'd want to join.

4. Patronize the arts

The campus is often home to cultural events that draw locals, as well as students. Click on Events, Museums, Arts, or a similar link to learn about the school's film screenings, plays, lectures, art shows, poetry readings, concerts, and other cultural events.

5. Learn about academic support

You'll find that colleges take great pains to keep you on campus once you get there. They offer a wide range of support services, which can include everything from drop-in writing assistance and peer tutoring to time management minicourses. You should find a description of these services in a section called Student Services or simply Students, but you might have to refer to the site map.

6. Check out the library

Find a link to the school's online library resources to learn how large the book collection is, and try out their online catalog. You can also learn how the library teaches new students about its services.

7. Grab a tray

While some campuses offer only school-run cafeterias, others rent space to private businesses selling everything from pizza to garden burgers. Look for a link to Dining Services and get a taste of what's available. You might even find this week's menu online.

8. Check into housing

You might be surprised at the many varieties of on-campus housing (go to "Choose Your Housing options" on page 201).

To find out what will be available to you during your first year, your best bet is to look for a Housing link under tabs for **Admissions** or **Prospective Students**. But to learn about future options, try looking under **Student Services** or **Current Students**.

9. Check up on student health services

You'll probably be charged a student health fee when you register for classes, so why not find out what you're paying for? Look for a link that will take you to the student health services section. You'll learn which medical and counseling services are included and which are not.

10. Log on to computing services

Do the dorm rooms have Wi-Fi? Can you buy a discounted laptop through the college? What technology support services does the college offer? Will you be able to register for classes online, or will you have to stand in line? For answers, look for an Information Technology link on the home page.

11. (So who's counting?) Root for the home team

Care for a set of tennis? A yoga class? Or maybe you're more at home cheering in the stands. Click on Athletics to look into intramural and recreational sports (in which any student can take part), fitness equipment and classes, and varsity season calendars.

10 Tips for Using Social Media

Just about every college can be found on social networking sites like Facebook, YouTube, or Twitter. Some colleges are even abandoning college fairs and relying solely on social media to reach students. Here are some tips to help you make the best use of it all.

1. Join college communities

Colleges provide social networking sites to connect current students, professors, admission officers, and prospective applicants like yourself. Joining these communities allows you to ask questions and get a sense of what it would be like to go there.

2. Go to the videotape

Student-made videos are a great way to get a sense of what a campus really looks and sounds like. YouTube's Education section has a fairly comprehensive list of colleges covered by such videos—and provides a good alternative when an actual visit is just not possible.

3. Follow the tweets

You can learn a lot from following a college on Twitter. Some colleges send tweet reminders, like when the acceptance deadline is due. But don't rely on tweeting to communicate with a college or to make an impression. For one thing, a college's tweets are usually generated by low-level staff, not decision-makers.

4. Don't friend college officials

Students use social media to communicate and connect with everyone, including colleges. But what are the rules? It's definitely not the same as connecting with friends and family. Few college officials would want to "friend" you, but in any event it's just not a good idea. Even if you are confident there is nothing embarrassing on your profile, you can't be sure how it might be interpreted by someone in that capacity.

5. Be careful about what you are posting

You've probably heard that some colleges monitor social media to check up on applicants and may even base a rejection on what they found on an applicant's social media profile or posting. (Employers do this too.) Don't let that scare you off Facebook, but it's a good idea to look at your page through the eyes of an admission officer. Sometimes images you think are innocent can be misinterpreted.

6. Don't put too much faith in matchmakers

Some sites, like Cappex for example, are "matchmakers." You create a profile on the site, and a program matches you to colleges that "fit" based on what the colleges tell the site they are looking for. This approach can lead to good colleges to explore, but don't rely on it to do your search for you or to build your final list of colleges. It just isn't that easy.

7. Don't take a chance on "chance me"

Beware of "chance me" sites where a "jury" of other students judge your chances of getting into a college. What you are really chancing is being discouraged by people who don't know what they are talking about. Leave your admission chances to the experts.

8. Learn what real students think, but remember they don't know it all

There are several popular social media sites like Niche or Unigo that provide student reviews and ratings of colleges. Sites like these can often give the unvarnished truth about the social scene or what the food is like.

But don't rely solely on student reviews or the opinions of your friends. It's not likely they can truly know what is best for you or steer you to all the best colleges, so keep your school counselor in the mix.

9. Save time with mashups and RSS feeds

It can take too long to do all this online research one school at a time. Social media mashup sites help by bringing together all the reviews, blogs, videos, and real-time tweets about a college into one place.

RSS feeds also help you to keep up; when you find a site you like, subscribe to the site's RSS feed, and you will be constantly notified of updates. This works especially well with blogs.

10. Keep coming back

Consistently following colleges online is a good way to see what they are like and if you can see yourself fitting in there. Over time, you gain insight into what is important to those colleges and if you are a good match.

Many students find that sites like Facebook work best after they have their short list of colleges and want to get more personalized information to help make final choices. After you've been accepted, social media are even more useful as a way to find classmates and begin to feel part of the school before showing up for orientation.

Basic Choices to Make

If you're just starting to think about what kind of college to look for, and are fairly open to all the possibilities, you might find it difficult to focus on what matters most. The best way to begin is to think about the really basic, fundamental choices first.

Below are brief outlines of the "big picture" elements you should consider.

Commute from home or live away

Either way, you can have a great college experience; but it will be a much different experience. Don't decide this on your own—talk to your family, friends, and anyone else you trust to give you both sides.

Location, location, location

This choice is usually among the first to make and most decisive. Do you want to be able to go home whenever you want, or would you rather experience a different part of the country? Are you excited by what a big city can offer, or do you need easy access to the outdoors or the serenity of a small town? Do you hate cold weather, enjoy the different seasons, need to be near a beach?

None of this has much to do with college itself, but a lot to do with how much you will enjoy it.

Four-year versus two-year

This choice probably depends on three things: what type of degree you are going for, how much you are willing or able to spend, and if you want to commute from home. Your local community college offers low-cost options for either vocational/technical training or the first two years of a four-year program. (For more info, see the "Community College Fact Sheet" on page 62.) "Junior" colleges are private two-year schools, and usually more expensive.

> When applying to a university, applicants typically have to choose a specific college or school division that they want to apply to. Each college may have its own admission requirements, and some may be more competitive than others.

Large, medium, or small?

This is more than the "big fish, little pond" question. Size can affect your options and experiences, such as the range of majors offered, the variety of student activities available, the amount of personal attention you'll receive, and the availability and size of facilities such as laboratories, libraries, and art studios. But remember, large universities are often broken up into small colleges or schools, so you can have it both ways…sort of.

College type

Choosing among these usually depends upon your career goals, and what type of college experience you want:

Liberal arts colleges emphasize the humanities, social sciences, and natural sciences, and the development of general knowledge and reasoning ability rather than specific career skills. Most are private, classes tend to be small, and you are likely to get more personal attention than in a large university. Examples: Amherst; Oberlin.

Universities are generally larger than colleges and offer more majors and research facilities. Most universities are subdivided into colleges or schools, such as a college of arts and sciences, a school of engineering, a business school, or a teacher's college (plus graduate schools). These subdivisions may all be on the same campus, or spread out over several different campuses. Examples: Rutgers, UCLA.

Agricultural, technical, and career colleges offer training for specific occupations or industries. Varieties include art schools and music conservatories, business colleges, schools of health science, and maritime colleges. Examples: Pratt, Kettering.

Religiously affiliated colleges are private colleges that are associated with a particular religious faith. The connection may range from being historic only, to being closely integrated into day-to-day student life. Examples: Boston College, Dallas Baptist U.

Historically black colleges originated in the time when African American students were denied access to most other colleges and universities. Their mission remains focused on the education of African Americans. Example: Spelman.

Hispanic-serving colleges are designated as such because Hispanic students comprise at least 25 percent of their full-time undergraduates. Example: Texas State University.

Majors and academic programs

If you have a clear idea of what you want to study, that obviously narrows your college choices to those that offer majors in that field. But if you're undecided (like most students), look for colleges that offer a broad range of majors and programs. That way you can reduce the chance that you'll have to transfer once you've made up your mind.

You might also want to consider a special study option that can enrich your experience, such as study abroad, cooperative education (where you work in the field as you learn), or an honors program. If experiences like these are important to you, make them part of your college search criteria.

Cost

Of course, cost is an important consideration for most students. But don't let "sticker shock" scare you away from colleges that might be a good fit. Financial aid often makes up the difference between what you can afford to pay and what a college costs. There are several calculators on collegeboard.org that will help you estimate the bottom line.

Accreditation: Must Knows

What is accreditation?

Think of it as a "seal of approval" that lets you know that a college meets quality standards established by an accrediting agency. The standards for each agency are slightly different but, in general, they set criteria for evaluating a college's administrative procedures, financial condition, physical facilities, and academic programs.

Types of accrediting agencies

Regional and national agencies examine the overall quality of the entire college as a whole. Specialized agencies accredit specific programs of study offered within a college, such as nursing, engineering, or teacher education. For example, ABET, Inc. (www.abet.org) accredits programs in applied science, computing, engineering, and technology, while AACSB International (www.aacsb.edu) accredits business and accounting programs.

You can find more information about accrediting agencies at the Council for Higher Education Accreditation's website (www.chea.org).

What does accreditation mean to me?

If you attend an accredited college, you can be sure that:

- Employers and professional licensing boards will recognize the degree you earn as an academic credential, as will graduate schools and other academic institutions you may apply to.

- You will be eligible for federal student aid to help pay for your costs, if you qualify based on financial need.

- Your tuition will qualify for federal income tax deductions and/or credits (if you meet other conditions).

- Academic credits you earn there are eligible to transfer to another accredited college.

- The college is financially sound and will likely still be in business when it's time to grant you a degree.

> Only colleges that are accredited by an agency recognized by the U.S. Department of Education may distribute federal financial aid to their students.

But there are some things accreditation doesn't mean:

- There's no guarantee that you will receive financial aid just because your college is accredited.

- Regional and national accreditation ensures that every academic program at the college meets standards, but that doesn't mean that the qualities of every program at the college are equal.

- If you want to transfer to another college, there's no guarantee that all your credits will count toward the graduation requirements of that college. If you plan to go to a community college for your first two years and then transfer to a four-year college, be sure to talk to a transfer counselor before enrolling in courses.

- Similarly, there's no guarantee that graduate schools or employers will see your undergraduate course of study as appropriate preparation for the demands of their particular program or job requirements.

> Every college contained in collegeboard.org's College Search has been accredited by either a national or regional accrediting agency recognized by the U.S. Department of Education.

Bottom line

One of the first things you should verify when you look at a college is its accreditation—especially if it has only been operating a few years. If you can't be completely confident that the degree you earn will be accepted as a bona fide credential (or that the college will still be in business when you graduate), look elsewhere.

Community College Fact Sheet

Community colleges are everywhere

Community colleges are the most geographically accessible institutions in the United States. Every state has at least one community college, and most have multiple colleges, with branch campuses and learning centers dotted throughout the state.

Community colleges are your least expensive option

While tuition and fees to attend a community college vary greatly from state to state, they are much lower than those charged by four-year colleges and universities. On average, the annual tuition and fees for a community college are about a third of what you would pay at most four-year colleges.

Almost half of all college students attend a community college

Collectively, community colleges in the United States enroll about 7.7 million students, comprising 45 percent of all students in higher education.

Community college students are more likely to work while attending college

Among all students attending a community college, more than two-thirds of them work; about equally divided between full-time and part-time employment.

Community colleges offer two kinds of learning

If English is your second language, community colleges have special programs that will help you build your English skills.

If your goal is a four-year degree, you can earn a two-year associate degree at a low-cost community college, then transfer to a four-year college as a junior.

If your goal is career training, you can earn an occupational degree or certificate in two years or less, then start working immediately in many high-demand fields (like health care or computer technology).

Community colleges can help you meet a range of academic goals

If you're achievement-oriented, community colleges offer challenging honors courses. You may be able to transfer directly into the honors program at a university, or at least make yourself a better candidate for it. Honors programs not only stimulate you but also offer mentoring and networking opportunities.

If you need more academic preparation, community college can offer a leg-up to achieving your goals. New students usually take placement tests in reading, writing, and math. Those who need to build skills can take catch-up courses, and then move into a regular academic program.

If your high school grades aren't the greatest, but a four-year college is your goal, taking community college courses—and building a record of good grades—can polish your academic record. Then you can transfer. (But don't expect it to be easy—community college courses are no different from four-year college courses.)

Researchers from the University of Illinois at Chicago and Penn State compared college grads from similar backgrounds who began college in two-year and in four-year institutions. On average, the two groups ended up with similar salaries, in careers that offered similar job prestige, stability, and satisfaction.

Community colleges allow you to learn on your schedule

Because many community college students have jobs and family responsibilities, community colleges tend to offer courses days, nights, and weekends. Some also offer courses online (distance learning); combine Internet and classroom learning; give interactive TV courses; condense semester courses into a shorter time frame; and more.

Seeking training for an occupation?

A community college may be the best route to many high-demand jobs that require two-year degrees or certificates not available at four-year colleges. Look for courses in computer technology, health care, paralegal studies, law enforcement, and biotechnology. With homeland security a constant concern, community colleges are training many first responders.

Your
College Major

Some students start college knowing exactly what they'd like to major in, but most do not. And almost half of all college students switch their majors at least once.

At this stage it's OK to be undecided. But you should think about your career goals and academic interests, at least in general terms, as you look at colleges and the majors they offer, so you can preserve your options.

Just what is a college major anyway?

Colleges (with few exceptions) require you to focus the bulk of your courses on a specific academic subject or field of study, in order to demonstrate sustained, high-level work in one field. That's your major.

You have plenty of time to decide

At most colleges, you aren't required to declare a major until the end of your sophomore year. If you're in a two-year degree program, you'll probably select a major at the start because your course of studies is much shorter.

How to choose

First, think about yourself. Think about what has interested you most, what you are good at, and how you like to spend your time. You will be most likely to enjoy and succeed at a course of study that incorporates some of these things. If you have definite career goals, find out which majors will lead you there. (See "Matching Careers to Degrees" on the next page.)

In your first year or two of college, you'll probably be required to take several introductory-level courses across a range of subjects. You will also be able to take a few elective courses that interest you. Use this period to explore your options with an open mind—you might be surprised to learn that you are fascinated by a subject you hadn't considered before.

As you consider majors, look outside the academic world as well. Get a realistic perspective of how graduates in these fields fare in the job market.

If you're still undecided about your college major, relax—just pick a college that offers a range of majors and programs, and take courses in subjects you find intriguing. Most colleges offer advising or mentoring to help you find a focus.

Seek advice

Remember, you're not alone. Choosing a major is usually done with the help of academic and peer advisers.

Matching Careers to Degrees

One of the best things about getting a college education is that you have more careers to choose from. Below you'll find some sample careers and the types of degrees they usually require.

TWO-YEAR ASSOCIATE DEGREE

Aircraft and avionics technician
Computer support specialists
Computer programmer
Crime scene investigator
Database administrator
Dental hygienist
Drafting technologist
Electrician
EMT Paramedic
Engineering technician
Game designer
Lab technician
Licensed practical nurse (LPN)
Optician
Paralegal
Preschool teacher
Physical therapy assistant
Radiologist (X-ray technician)
Restaurant manager
Veterinary technician

FOUR-YEAR BACHELOR'S DEGREE

Accountant
Advanced nurse practitioner
Airline pilot
Animator
Civil engineer
Clinical laboratory technologist
Computer engineer
Computer systems analyst
Construction manager
Dietician
Financial adviser
Forester
Graphic designer
Hotel manager
Journalist
Landscape architect
Park ranger
Physician assistant
Registered nurse (RN)
Social worker
Software developer
Teacher
Webmaster
Wildlife manager

GRADUATE DEGREE

Archaeologist
Architect
Astronomer
College professor
Dentist
Doctor
Economist
Forensic scientist
Genetic engineer
Lawyer
Librarian
Microbiologist
Museum curator
Pharmacist
Physical therapist
Psychologist
Research scientist
Statistician
Veterinarian

Step-by-Step
Career Worksheet

You don't have to have your whole life figured out before you can search for colleges. But it does help to have some basic idea of what career paths might interest you as you consider the courses and majors that colleges offer. This worksheet will help you focus your thinking.

STEP 1: THINK ABOUT WHAT INTERESTS YOU

Start with a real basic inventory of what you are curious about (nature, different countries, machinery?), how you like to spend your time (alone, with people, outdoors, reading?), and what makes you happy (working with your hands, helping others, cooking?). It also helps to remember what you don't like—that tells you a lot about yourself too.

WHAT I'M CURIOUS ABOUT:

HOW I LIKE TO SPEND MY TIME:

MY LIKES AND DISLIKES:

STEP 2: TRANSLATE THE ABOVE INTO JOB IDEAS

Take a general area of interest, such as working with kids, then come up with jobs that fall into that category. Make a question-and-answer game of it. ("How many jobs involve animals?") Need help? Think about people you've read about or met who have interesting jobs, or use the career quizzes that are available in your counselor's office or online.

INTEREST	JOB IDEAS
INTEREST	JOB IDEAS
INTEREST	JOB IDEAS

STEP 3: CONSIDER HOW TO GET THERE

Now think about what kinds of classes or special degrees you might need to get the jobs that sound good to you. You might find you don't like any of the classes you'd need to take, for example, which would certainly tell you something. To get information about education requirements for different jobs, go to "Majors and Careers" on collegeboard.org.

JOB IDEA	JOB REQUIREMENTS
JOB IDEA	JOB REQUIREMENTS
JOB IDEA	JOB REQUIREMENTS

STEP 4: GIVE IT A WHIRL

Once you focus on possible jobs, try to really dive into them:

• Volunteer somewhere that's in a similar field.

• Look into a paid or unpaid internship.

• Shadow someone to see a day-in-the-life.

• Research, by visiting your library or useful website.

Even if you decide not to pursue a related career, you'll have gained valuable experience and given your college application a boost.

THINGS I COULD DO RIGHT NOW

Four "Top 10" Career Charts

Wondering where the jobs will be in the future? Government economists have estimated which occupations and industries will grow the fastest, and which occupations will have the most new jobs.

As you think about majors, check out the following "Top 10" lists to see what's hot.

Top 10 industries with the fastest employment growth

INDUSTRY	PERCENT INCREASE 2014–2024
Health care	21%
Construction	13%
Education	10%
Management, business, and professional services	10%
Mining	10%
Leisure and hospitality	6%
Financial services	6%
Retail and wholesale trade	6%
State and local government	4%
Transportation and warehousing	3%

Top 10 fastest-growing occupations for college grads

OCCUPATION	PERCENT INCREASE 2014–2024
Personal financial advisors	30%
Cartographers and geographers	29%
Interpreters and translators	29%
Forensic science technicians	27%
Biomedical engineers	23%
Computer system analysts	21%
Athletic trainers	21%
Market research analysts	19%
Insurance adjusters and actuaries	18%
Licensed practical nurses	16%

Top 10 occupations with the most job openings for four-year college grads

OCCUPATION	TOTAL JOB OPENINGS 2014–2024
Registered nurses	1,088,000
Business, sales, and operations managers	797,000
Elementary and middle-school teachers	554,000
Accountants and auditors	500,000
Computer systems analysts	366,000
High school teachers	284,000
Engineers	282,000
Financial managers and analysts	259,000
Market research analysts	151,000
Medical and health services managers	141,000

Top 10 occupations with the most job openings for two-year college grads

OCCUPATION	TOTAL JOB OPENINGS 2014–2024
Medical and health technologists	194,000
Pre-school teachers	159,000
Engineering technologists	112,000
Paralegals	83,000
Occupational and physical therapy assistants	78,000
Dental hygienists	70,000
Web developers	59,000
Computer network support specialists	37,000
Veterinarian technicians/assistants	27,000
Drafters and surveyors	20,000

Source: United States Bureau of Labor Statistics

ROTC FAQs

Are you attracted to the idea of military service? Are you also looking for ways to finance college on your own? The answers below will explain how to achieve both.

What is ROTC?

The Reserve Officers' Training Corps (ROTC) prepares young men and women to become military officers while they attend college. There are both scholarship and nonscholarship programs available for each branch: Army, Navy, Air Force, and Marines. While you attend college, you'll take some military courses each year for credit, and attend training sessions. After you finish college, you must complete a period of service in the military.

Who is eligible for an ROTC scholarship?

The scholarships are based on merit, not need. To qualify you must:

- Be a U.S. citizen
- Be between the ages of 17 and 26
- Have a high school GPA of at least 2.5
- Have a high school diploma
- Meet physical standards
- Agree to accept a commission and serve in the military on active duty or in the Reserves after graduating
- Achieve a qualifying score on either the SAT or ACT

How much money do ROTC scholarships offer?

Scholarship amounts vary by program, but can go up to full tuition and fees. Room and board are not covered. You also receive money each year for books and a monthly allowance.

How much time do I owe the military after I complete ROTC?

Most cadets incur a four-year active-duty commitment, but it can be longer depending upon the military path you pursue. For example, pilots in the Air Force incur a 10-year active-duty service commitment.

What if I don't like ROTC?

You can quit the program after your first year without any obligations. After that you'll have to pay any scholarship money back.

What kinds of courses and training does ROTC offer?

It varies by branch, but generally you take one military science course per semester. In addition, you'll wear a uniform once a week during military labs, drills, and other practical training activities. Most programs also require participation in at least one summer program—such as midshipmen cruises in Naval ROTC—to round out your military training.

Will I have a choice of major?

Most ROTC students can choose any major they want. But sometimes a particular branch of the military may only offer scholarships in those majors that meet the needs of that branch.

Where is ROTC offered?

It varies college by college. You can find schools that have the ROTC program you want on collegeboard.org.

College Fair Tip Sheet

College fairs may not have peanuts, popcorn, and pony rides, but they can be very informative and even fun. Fairs can help you rule out colleges, as well as introduce you to new ones.

You'll find noise and crowds at most college fairs, and it can be a little overwhelming. So, here's a plan for before, during, and after you go.

Before the Fair

Think about what you want

The whole point of a college fair is to ask questions. Make a list of what's important to you. (See the "What You Want Checklist" on page 78.) Then you'll know what to ask about.

What to bring

You'll need a pen and small notebook, your questions, and a bag to hold all the college brochures and information you'll get.

During the Fair

Go early

That's the best way to avoid crowds. Plan to talk first to the colleges that interest you most; that way you won't miss out if they get jammed later. Local colleges and your state universities usually attract a lot of visitors, so hit them early if you want to check them out.

Don't just wander around

Navigating a large college fair can be challenging. Here are some ways to create some beelines to what you want to see:

- Review the list of colleges at the fair and identify the colleges that interest you.
- If the fair provides a map showing where college booths will be, plan out a route to avoid backtracking.
- If the fair has information sessions with experts (e.g., about financial aid), block out time for the ones you want to attend.

Fly solo

It might be more fun to go around with your friends, but you won't get much accomplished. Alone, the college rep will be able to focus on you one-on-one, and you'll be free to ask questions.

Take notes

After you visit a college's booth, take a few minutes to jot down what you've learned (you can use the journal pages starting on page 73). Otherwise it will all become a blur, and you won't remember which college said what.

Be curious

Try to leave some time at the end just to browse through some of the booths you didn't get to—you could stumble on a great college you hadn't considered.

After the Fair

Don't forget about it

Don't lose the college materials in the back of your closet. Look through what you brought back, and your notes, within the week. But don't keep everything: Weed out colleges that aren't a good fit.

Follow up

Research colleges that interest you. Explore their websites, request more information from admission offices, and plan to visit.

20 Questions to Ask College Reps

Whether you meet them at a college fair or on a campus visit, college reps genuinely enjoy talking to high school students and answering questions about their college. While you shouldn't expect them to reveal any negative info, they can be a good source for what you need to know. The following questions will help start a good dialogue:

1. What makes your college unique?

2. What academic programs is your college most known for?

3. How would you describe the kids that go there? Where do most of them come from?

4. Where do kids hang out on campus?

5. What happens on weekends—are there things to do on campus or in town, or do most kids go home?

6. Are fraternities and sororities a big part of campus life?

7. What are the housing options for freshmen?

8. Do many students live off campus?

9. Is there a sports complex or fitness center?

10. What are the most popular clubs and activities?

11. What's the security like on campus?

12. What's the surrounding area like? Is it easy to get around?

13. What are the most popular majors?

14. How would you describe the academic pressure and workload?

15. What support services are available (academic advisers, tutors, etc.)?

16. Is the campus Wi-Fi?

17. What's the faculty like? How accessible are they outside of class?

18. Are there opportunities for internships?

19. Is there job placement help for graduates?

20. Are any big changes in the works that I should know about?

College Fair Journal

COLLEGE 1	COLLEGE 2
Name	Name
Location	Location
Name of Rep	Name of Rep
Did I fill out a card? ☐ Yes ☐ No	Did I fill out a card? ☐ Yes ☐ No
Still Interested? ☐ Yes ☐ No	Still Interested? ☐ Yes ☐ No
Reasons Why	Reasons Why
Reasons Why Not	Reasons Why Not
What Impressed Me the Most	What Impressed Me the Most

College Fair Journal

COLLEGE 3

Name

Location

Name of Rep

Did I fill out a card? ☐ Yes ☐ No

Still Interested? ☐ Yes ☐ No

Reasons Why

Reasons Why Not

What Impressed Me the Most

COLLEGE 4

Name

Location

Name of Rep

Did I fill out a card? ☐ Yes ☐ No

Still Interested? ☐ Yes ☐ No

Reasons Why

Reasons Why Not

What Impressed Me the Most

College Fair Journal

COLLEGE 5	COLLEGE 6

COLLEGE 5

Name
_____

Location
_____

Name of Rep
_____

Did I fill out a card? ☐ Yes ☐ No

Still Interested? ☐ Yes ☐ No

Reasons Why
_____
_____
_____
_____
_____
_____

Reasons Why Not
_____
_____
_____

What Impressed Me the Most
_____
_____
_____
_____

COLLEGE 6

Name
_____

Location
_____

Name of Rep
_____

Did I fill out a card? ☐ Yes ☐ No

Still Interested? ☐ Yes ☐ No

Reasons Why
_____
_____
_____
_____
_____
_____

Reasons Why Not
_____
_____
_____

What Impressed Me the Most
_____
_____
_____
_____

College Fair Journal

<table>
<tr><td>

COLLEGE 7

Name

Location

Name of Rep

Did I fill out a card? ☐ Yes ☐ No

Still Interested? ☐ Yes ☐ No

Reasons Why

Reasons Why Not

What Impressed Me the Most

</td><td>

COLLEGE 8

Name

Location

Name of Rep

Did I fill out a card? ☐ Yes ☐ No

Still Interested? ☐ Yes ☐ No

Reasons Why

Reasons Why Not

What Impressed Me the Most

</td></tr>
</table>

College Fair Journal

COLLEGE 9	COLLEGE 10
Name	Name
Location	Location
Name of Rep	Name of Rep
Did I fill out a card? ☐ Yes ☐ No	Did I fill out a card? ☐ Yes ☐ No
Still Interested? ☐ Yes ☐ No	Still Interested? ☐ Yes ☐ No
Reasons Why	Reasons Why
Reasons Why Not	Reasons Why Not
What Impressed Me the Most	What Impressed Me the Most

What You Want Checklist

Use this checklist to create a picture of what your ideal college would look like. Rate each component so that you can weigh how close each college comes to your ideal. Then use the results to come up with your "short list" of colleges.

LOCATION	Must be	Like to be
Commuting distance	☐	☐
Not too far from home	☐	☐
Far from home	☐	☐
Specific state/city	☐	☐

ENVIRONMENT	Must be	Like to be
Big city	☐	☐
Small city	☐	☐
Suburbs	☐	☐
College town	☐	☐
Rural	☐	☐
Mountains	☐	☐
By the sea	☐	☐
Warm all year	☐	☐

TYPE OF COLLEGE	Must be	Like to be
Four-year	☐	☐
Two-year	☐	☐
Religiously affiliated	☐	☐
Single-sex	☐	☐
University	☐	☐
Liberal arts	☐	☐
Art/music school	☐	☐
Technical	☐	☐
Other: _____	☐	☐

SIZE OF COLLEGE	Must be	Like to be
Small	☐	☐
Medium	☐	☐
Large	☐	☐

CAMPUS	Must be	Like to be
Traditional	☐	☐
Modern	☐	☐
Parklike	☐	☐

ACADEMIC OFFERINGS	Must have	Like to have
Many majors	☐	☐
Specific majors:		
_____	☐	☐
_____	☐	☐
_____	☐	☐
Teacher certification	☐	☐
ROTC	☐	☐
Study abroad	☐	☐
Co-op program	☐	☐
Internships	☐	☐
Other: _____	☐	☐

FACILITIES	Must have	Like to have
Design/visual arts center	☐	☐
Music/performing arts center	☐	☐
Sports/fitness center	☐	☐
Science center	☐	☐
Tech center	☐	☐
Health center	☐	☐
TV/radio station	☐	☐
Other: _____	☐	☐

HOUSING	Must have	Like to have
On campus	☐	☐
Off campus	☐	☐
Quiet	☐	☐
Special interest/theme	☐	☐
Single-sex	☐	☐
Substance-free	☐	☐
Fraternity/sorority	☐	☐

ACTIVITIES	Must have	Like to have
Intramural/club sports	☐	☐
Specific sport(s):		
_____	☐	☐
_____	☐	☐
_____	☐	☐
Religious clubs	☐	☐
Minority/ethnic clubs	☐	☐
Theater	☐	☐
Band/orchestra	☐	☐
Dance	☐	☐
Newspaper/journal	☐	☐
Other: _____	☐	☐

SERVICES	Must have	Like to have
Job/internship placement	☐	☐
Career counseling	☐	☐
Health	☐	☐
ESL	☐	☐
Services for disabled/impaired	☐	☐

Your Short List of Colleges

OK—this is the result of all your research so far: the colleges you most likely will apply to. You should have 1 or 2 "reaches," 2 to 4 "probables," and 1 or 2 "safeties." Ideally, every college on this list will be a good fit.

	COLLEGE 1	COLLEGE 2	COLLEGE 3
NAME OF COLLEGE			
How hard is it to get in? (Reach/Probable/Safety)			
What I like most			
What I don't like			
Majors offered that I'm interested in			
What's unique (campus features, interesting facilities, or programs)			
Sports, clubs, or activities offered that I'm interested in			
Costs • Tuition & fees • Room & board • Travel			
Estimated Financial Aid • Scholarships/grants • Loans/work study			

COLLEGE 4	COLLEGE 5	COLLEGE 6	COLLEGE 7	COLLEGE 8

Visiting
Colleges

When to Visit Colleges

Schoolwork, your job, your parents…it can be tough to find the right time to go on campus visits. But try not to lose sight of the reason you're going: to see if the school is a good fit for you. That means you want to go when the college is in session, so you can see the place in action.

During the week is best

Mondays through Thursdays are ideal since campuses are generally in full swing. If it's not possible to take time off from school or work, try to visit during holidays that fall on Mondays, when most colleges are in session.

Spring of junior year

Juniors who have researched colleges should consider using spring vacations for college visits. Spring is also a good time of year if you play fall sports or are considering Early Action or Early Decision with application deadlines in November of senior year.

> Summertime may not be the best time because campuses are usually deserted; but it might be the only time you can go. If that's the case, check to see if tours are available (they usually are) or if there is a summer session.

After you've been accepted

Many colleges invite their accepted candidates to spend a few days on campus before the May 1 reply date to encourage them to enroll. This is a good opportunity to nail down your final choice.

The best practice is to visit colleges before you apply, so that you're confident you'd be happy at any of the colleges on your list.

Times to avoid

Check specific dates with each college so you don't arrive at a bad time:

• When the admission office is closed to visitors

• Exam periods

• Graduation week

• Move-in day

Based on information found in *Campus Visits & College Interviews*, by Zola Dincin Schneider

Campus Visit Checklist

Here are things you shouldn't miss while visiting a college. Take a look at this list before you go to make sure that you allow enough time to get a sense of what the school is really like.

☐ Take a campus tour.

☐ Have an interview with an admission officer.

☐ Get business cards and names of people you meet for future contacts.

☐ Pick up financial aid forms.

☐ Participate in a group information session at the admission office.

☐ Sit in on a class of a subject that interests you.

☐ Talk to a professor in your chosen major or in a subject that interests you.

☐ Talk to coaches of sports in which you might participate.

☐ Talk to a student or counselor in the career center.

☐ Spend the night in a dorm.

☐ Grab the student newspaper.

☐ Try to find other student publications—department newsletters, alternative newspapers, literary reviews.

☐ Scan bulletin boards to see what day-to-day student life is like.

☐ Eat in the cafeteria.

☐ Ask students how they like it here. (See "Questions to Ask During the Visit" on the next page.)

☐ Wander around the campus by yourself for a while.

☐ Browse in the college bookstore.

☐ Walk or drive around the community surrounding the campus.

☐ Listen to the college's radio station.

☐ Try to see a dorm that you didn't see on the tour.

Based on information found in *Campus Visits & College Interviews*, by Zola Dincin Schneider

Questions to Ask During the Visit

You won't find out much from just walking around looking at the buildings. Make the trip worthwhile by asking questions. These lists give you plenty to choose from:

Questions to ask students:

1. Has going here turned out like you expected? Any surprises or disappointments?

2. What are the best reasons to go here?

3. What do students complain about?

4. I have to choose a dorm. What can you tell me about the choices?

5. If you could do it over again, would you still choose to go here?

6. What kind of meal plan makes the most sense?

7. What is there to do off campus? Is it easy to get around?

8. What do most students do for fun on weekends?

9. How often do students go home on weekends?

10. Where do most students hang out on campus?

11. Can you study in the dorms? If not, where do you go to study?

12. Do you use the library often? Is it easy to find what you need there?

13. How's the bookstore? Can you find the books you need there? Is it easy to get used textbooks?

14. How is the campus network? Does it go down often?

15. I know it depends on your major, but in general, what's the workload like?

16. How are the professors? Are they hard to reach outside of class?

17. Is it easy to get the classes you want?

18. How would you rate the courses you've taken so far?

19. Would you characterize this college as mostly liberal, conservative, or open-minded?

20. Do you get much help finding internships or jobs?

21. Do most students join fraternities/sororities? Are you out of it if you aren't in one?

22. Is there much of a drug scene?

23. Do I have to worry about things getting stolen?

24. Is the campus safe at night?

25. How would you describe the relationship between students and the administration?

Questions to ask the tour guide:

1. How popular is the recreation/sports/fitness center? Is it crowded often?

2. Where do you do laundry? Is it convenient? Will I need to hoard quarters?

3. Is there any overcrowding in the dorms (three students in a double, for example)?

4. Do many resident students have cars? Is there enough parking?

5. I'm thinking of majoring in _____. What relevant facilities should I see?

6. Where can you get something to eat after the cafeteria is closed?

7. How large are most classes? Do many take place in auditoriums?

8. What are the most popular extracurricular activities?

9. Are there many intramural or club sports?

10. Are there enough computers, printers, and copying machines available? What about at night?

11. Does student government play much of a role on campus?

Questions to ask at the admission office:

1. When does registration take place for freshmen? What is the registration procedure?

2. Do freshmen have to take any placement exams?

3. What sort of job placement or career counseling is available before graduation?

4. How much should I expect tuition to increase over the next four years?

5. Who should I speak to about financial aid? (See "10 Questions for the Financial Aid Office" on page 172.)

6. Is there a course catalog I can take with me?

Based on information found in *Campus Visits & College Interviews*, by Zola Dincin Schneider

Sizing Up a Dorm Checklist

If you plan to live on campus, try to learn the following from a campus visit, talking to students, or visits to the school's website.

Dorm facilities

☐ How are the rooms furnished? Do students have the option of changing the furniture—for example, constructing lofts for their beds?

☐ Are there kitchen facilities? Are students allowed to have appliances such as mini-refrigerators or microwave ovens in their rooms?

☐ Is there a laundry room in the dorm or close by?

☐ Is there a central lounge area? Does it have a TV, pool table, or anything else for fun?

☐ Are there computer labs in or near the dorms? Do the dorm rooms have Wi-Fi?

☐ What sort of telephone service is available in the dorms?

☐ Do the dorms get good cell phone reception?

☐ How well maintained are the halls and bathrooms?

Academic and social atmosphere

☐ Do the students seem friendly? Do they greet you as a visitor?

☐ Do students study together in the dorms?

☐ When students are in their rooms, do they leave their doors open, or do they close them?

☐ If the dorm has a lounge area, is it used much?

☐ How do students spend their weeknight evenings—do they hang out together in the dorms, or do they avoid the dorms at all costs?

Safety

☐ Are the pathways, bus stops, parking lots, and other public areas well lit at night?

☐ Are there emergency phones (connecting directly to the police) outside the dorms?

☐ Is theft a problem in the dorms?

☐ Are there security systems in place to prevent nonresidents from walking into a residence hall? Are ground-floor windows in the residence halls secured?

☐ Do campus security guards or local police patrol the campus?

Campus Visit Journal

COLLEGE

Date of visit

Location

Weather that day

	WHAT I LIKE	WHAT I DON'T LIKE
Campus		
Dorms		
Dining areas/food		
Activities available		
Course offerings		
Academic facilities		
Fitness/rec facilities		
Neighboring area		
Other		

PEOPLE I MET

Name   E-mail:

Name   E-mail:

Name   E-mail:

Name   E-mail:

What the students are like

What impressed me the most

SHOULD I GO HERE?

Campus Visit Journal

COLLEGE

Date of visit

Location

Weather that day

	WHAT I LIKE	WHAT I DON'T LIKE
Campus		
Dorms		
Dining areas/food		
Activities available		
Course offerings		
Academic facilities		
Fitness/rec facilities		
Neighboring area		
Other		

PEOPLE I MET

Name   E-mail:

Name   E-mail:

Name   E-mail:

Name   E-mail:

What the students are like

What impressed me the most

SHOULD I GO HERE?

Campus Visit Journal

Date of visit

Location

Weather that day

	WHAT I LIKE	WHAT I DON'T LIKE
Campus		
Dorms		
Dining areas/food		
Activities available		
Course offerings		
Academic facilities		
Fitness/rec facilities		
Neighboring area		
Other		

PEOPLE I MET

Name   E-mail:

Name   E-mail:

Name   E-mail:

Name   .   E-mail:

What the students are like

What impressed me the most

SHOULD I GO HERE?

Campus Visit Journal

COLLEGE

Date of visit

Location

Weather that day

	WHAT I LIKE	WHAT I DON'T LIKE
Campus		
Dorms		
Dining areas/food		
Activities available		
Course offerings		
Academic facilities		
Fitness/rec facilities		
Neighboring area		
Other		

PEOPLE I MET

Name   E-mail:

Name   E-mail:

Name   E-mail:

Name   E-mail:

What the students are like

What impressed me the most

SHOULD I GO HERE?

Campus Visit Journal

COLLEGE

Date of visit

Location

Weather that day

	WHAT I LIKE	WHAT I DON'T LIKE
Campus		
Dorms		
Dining areas/food		
Activities available		
Course offerings		
Academic facilities		
Fitness/rec facilities		
Neighboring area		
Other		

PEOPLE I MET

Name   E-mail:

Name   E-mail:

Name   E-mail:

Name   E-mail:

What the students are like

What impressed me the most

SHOULD I GO HERE?

Campus Visit Journal

COLLEGE

Date of visit

Location

Weather that day

	WHAT I LIKE	WHAT I DON'T LIKE
Campus		
Dorms		
Dining areas/food		
Activities available		
Course offerings		
Academic facilities		
Fitness/rec facilities		
Neighboring area		
Other		

PEOPLE I MET

Name   E-mail:

Name   E-mail:

Name   E-mail:

Name   E-mail:

What the students are like

What impressed me the most

SHOULD I GO HERE?

Campus Visit Journal

COLLEGE

Date of visit

Location

Weather that day

	WHAT I LIKE	WHAT I DON'T LIKE
Campus		
Dorms		
Dining areas/food		
Activities available		
Course offerings		
Academic facilities		
Fitness/rec facilities		
Neighboring area		
Other		

PEOPLE I MET

Name   E-mail:

Name   E-mail:

Name   E-mail:

Name   E-mail:

What the students are like

What impressed me the most

SHOULD I GO HERE?

Campus Visit Journal

COLLEGE

Date of visit

Location

Weather that day

	WHAT I LIKE	WHAT I DON'T LIKE
Campus		
Dorms		
Dining areas/food		
Activities available		
Course offerings		
Academic facilities		
Fitness/rec facilities		
Neighboring area		
Other		

PEOPLE I MET

Name   E-mail:

Name   E-mail:

Name   E-mail:

Name   E-mail:

What the students are like

What impressed me the most

SHOULD I GO HERE?

Taking Tests

FAQs About the PSAT/NMSQT®

1. What does PSAT/NMSQT stand for?

Preliminary SAT/National Merit Scholarship Qualifying Test.

2. Why should I take the PSAT/NMSQT?

The PSAT/NMSQT is great practice for the SAT, and it might qualify you for a National Merit Scholarship. Most important, the PSAT/NMSQT gives valuable feedback to you and your school. A question-by-question review of answers enables you to see which answers you got right, with explanations for the answers available on collegeboard.org.

3. What should I do to prepare for this test?

The best preparation is to do a lot of reading and writing, practice your math skills, and to become familiar with the test so you know what to expect. An official PSAT/NMSQT practice test can be downloaded from collegeboard.org. The *PSAT/NMSQT Student Guide* contains plenty of useful information, including a full-length practice test.

You can also go to Khan Academy® (satpractice. org) for free, interactive and personalized practice programs developed with actual test items from the College Board. Because of the close alignment of the tests, that will also help you prepare for the PSAT/NMSQT.

4. If I don't do well on this test, will that hurt my chances of getting into college?

Absolutely not. PSAT/NMSQT scores are not sent to colleges. If anything, taking the PSAT/NMSQT will improve your chances of going to college since the test provides information on skills that need improvement in preparation for the SAT and college.

5. How many times can I take this test?

Only once a year, but you can take it in multiple years if your school offers it to both sophomores and juniors. It is important to take the test in order to enter National Merit Scholarship Corporation competitions, as well as to prepare for the SAT. For younger students, the main benefit is to gain valuable feedback, get a head start on improving their academic skills, and plan for college.

6. When should I expect to see my scores?

Your school will receive your score report in December and will notify you regarding when, where, and how to get your report.

7. What is in the PSAT/NMSQT Score Report?

The score report not only includes your scores and itemized feedback on test questions, but also personalized skills feedback and guidance on which areas to focus. The score report also shows whether you meet entry requirements for National Merit Scholarship Corporation competitions. You will also receive access to a personalized online college and career exploration tool to chart your path to college and beyond.

FAQs About AP Exams

Can I take the AP Exam if I haven't taken the AP course?

Yes. The College Board is committed to providing access to AP Exams to all students, including those who are home schooled or attend schools that do not offer AP courses. If you are one of those students or studying independently, contact the school counselor or AP Coordinator at a school that offers AP Exams to see if you can take the exam there.

Why should I take an AP Exam if I'm not looking to earn college credit or placement?

AP Exams provide colleges and universities with additional information about your ability to succeed in college-level study. Many colleges use AP Exam scores to place students into honors classes. Additionally, some scholarship programs consider AP Exam scores.

I have a disability. Are testing accommodations available?

If you have a documented disability, you may be eligible for accommodations on AP Exams. To find out more, visit collegeboard.org/ssd or contact your school's AP Coordinator.

If I don't get a good score on an AP Exam, will it hurt my chances for college admission?

Not likely. For one thing, it's your choice whether to report an AP Exam score to a college. But before you make that choice, consider this: Overall, nearly 60 percent of all AP test-takers receive AP scores of at least 3, which is regarded as a good indicator of your ability to do well in college. And any AP score tells colleges that you chose to take a difficult course and exam, and that you are serious about your studies.

How much time does it take to complete an AP Exam?

Most of the exams take two to three hours to complete. For subjects that correspond to a half-year college course, the exam is closer to two hours in length.

How are multiple-choice questions scored? Should I guess?

Your score on the multiple-choice section is based on the number of questions you answer correctly. No points are deducted for incorrect answers or unanswered questions.

Random guessing is unlikely to raise or lower your score much, but an educated guess based on eliminating obviously wrong answer choices is usually to your advantage.

What should I bring to the exam?

- Several sharpened No. 2 pencils with erasers for all multiple-choice questions.
- Pens with black or dark blue ink for free-response questions in most exams.
- Your six-digit school code. Home-schooled students will be given a code at the time of the exam.
- A watch (but without a beeper or alarm).
- An approved calculator if you're taking the AP Biology, Calculus, Chemistry, Physics, or Statistics Exams. Visit collegeboard.org to find the calculator policy for your subject.
- A ruler or straightedge if you're taking an AP Physics Exam.
- A photo ID if you do not attend the school where you are taking the exam.
- If you are eligible for testing accommodations, your SSD Student Accommodation Letter.

FAQs
About the SAT®

Why should I take the SAT?

Course content and grading standards vary widely among high schools. Entrance exams like the SAT help colleges compare applicants on a level playing field. The SAT is accepted by all U.S. colleges, and is also used by many scholarship programs. The SAT was recently redesigned to better reflect what students are learning in class, with a focus on the knowledge and skills students need for college. The SAT is also the only test that provides free, official practice tools for every single student.

When should I take the SAT?

Most students take the SAT during their junior or senior year in high school. Often, a student takes the SAT as a junior during the spring and retests the next fall. However, there are no age or grade restrictions for taking the test.

How do I register for the SAT?

The best way to register is online. It's fast and easy, and it helps you avoid late fees or missed postmark deadlines. You can even register for next year's tests over the summer. SAT registration may be completed at sat.org.

What if I can't afford the fee?

Fee waivers are available to high school juniors and seniors who cannot afford the test fee. To learn more visit sat.org/fee-waivers; you can also apply for fee waivers through your school counselor.

How long is the SAT?

The total testing time for the SAT is 3 hours, plus 50 minutes for the optional essay. You'll have 65 minutes for the Reading Test, 35 minutes for the Writing and Language Test, and 80 minutes for the Math Test.

Can I bring something to eat or drink during the test?

Students are encouraged to bring snacks in a book bag on test day. These snacks should be easily stowed under desks or chairs in the test room and can only be consumed in designated areas during breaks.

What will I be asked to do on the SAT?

The redesigned SAT requires you to:

- Analyze, revise and edit texts
- Understand vocabulary in context
- Use evidence to support your answers
- Use math to solve problems in science, social studies, and career-related contexts
- Analyze data and interpret tables and graphs

Will I be tested in subjects like science and social studies?

You will not be asked any subject-specific questions, such as "what is the Magna Carta." But you will be asked to apply your reading, writing, English, and math skills to answer questions and solve problems grounded in science, history, and social studies contexts.

How is vocabulary tested?

Vocabulary is tested through questions about the meaning of words and phrases in the context of prose passages that demonstrate how word choice shapes meaning, tone, and impact. The meaning of these words and phrases is derived in large part through the context; they are familiar words, but their meaning can shift depending on how and where they're used.

What math will be tested?

The math section covers four content areas:

- Heart of Algebra, which focuses on the mastery of linear equations and systems.
- Problem Solving and Data Analysis, which involves using ratios, percentages, and proportional reasoning to solve problems in science, social science, and career contexts.
- Passport to Advanced Math, which requires the manipulation of complex equations such as quadratic or exponential functions.
- Additional Topics in Math, which covers geometric and trigonometric skills.

Can I use a calculator on the Math Test?

The SAT Math test has two sections: one that allows calculators, and one that doesn't. Calculators are important mathematical tools, but the no-calculator section makes it easier to assess students' understanding of math concepts.

Should I plan to take the optional essay?

You don't have to take the SAT with Essay, but if you do, you'll be able to apply to colleges that recommend or require it. If you haven't chosen your schools yet, taking the essay will keep your college options open.

Can I get more detailed information about my scores?

You'll have access to a free, detailed online score report on collegeboard.org. There you will see the types of questions, level of difficulty, and how many in each group of questions you answered correctly, incorrectly, or omitted. You'll also be able to compare your scores with other groups of test-takers. If applicable, you can also access a copy of your essay.

What is Score Choice™?

If you take the SAT more than once, Score Choice allows you to choose which scores to send to your target colleges. All section scores from the selected test date will be reported, including the Essay score if you have one (you can't cherry-pick your best section scores from multiple test dates). Score Choice is optional; if you don't use it, all of your scores will be sent automatically.

Is the test fair to all students?

Yes. The test is straightforward, with no tricks designed to trip you up. And now it's easier than ever for students to show their best work. The College Board and Khan Academy® have partnered to provide personalized practice resources entirely free of charge, so every student, regardless of background, can have access to the best exam practice available.

Where can I learn more?

Go to sat.org for sample questions and more information.

The SAT
at a Glance

EVIDENCE-BASED READING AND WRITING

Reading Test	• 65 minutes, 52 questions (all multiple choice)
	• 4 single and 1 pair of reading passages; some will contain graphics (tables, charts, etc.)
	• 3 content areas (subject knowledge not tested): literature; history/social studies; science
Writing and Language Test	• 35 minutes, 44 questions (all multiple choice); 1 or more graphics in 1 or more sets of questions
	• 4 reading passages of 3 types: argument, informative/explanatory, nonfiction narrative
	• 4 content areas (subject knowledge not tested): careers; history/social studies; humanities; science
Total time	100 minutes
Score	200–800

MATHEMATICS

Calculator Section	• 55 minutes, 38 questions (30 multiple choice, 8 grid-in)
	• 4 content areas: Heart of Algebra, Problem Solving and Data Analysis, Passport to Advanced Math, Additional Topics in Math
No-Calculator Section	• 25 minutes, 20 questions (15 multiple choice, 5 grid-in)
	• 3 content areas: Heart of Algebra, Passport to Advanced Math, Additional Topics in Math
Total time	80 minutes
Score	200–800

ESSAY (OPTIONAL)

Based on the text of an argument written for a broad audience, you will be asked to consider how the author uses:

- evidence, such as facts or examples, to support claims
- reasoning to develop ideas and to connect claims and evidence
- stylistic/persuasive elements (word choice, tone, etc.), to add power to the ideas expressed

Time	50 minutes
Score	2 to 8 on each of three categories: reading, analysis, and writing

Practice for Free

The College Board has partnered with Khan Academy® to provide free, world-class online practice for all students. That means you can be as well-prepared as anyone, at no cost.

A personalized study plan

Official SAT Practice on Khan Academy is tailored for you, focusing on exactly what you need to practice the most. You can connect your College Board and Khan Academy accounts to create a personalized study plan based on your PSAT and/or SAT test results, so you can focus on the areas where you need the most work.

What you'll get

These are some of the resources you can access:

- Thousands of interactive problems with instant feedback
- Video lessons that explain problems step-by-step and give you study and test-taking tips
- Plenty of full-length practice tests
- A personalized study schedule to help you stay on track and plan for test day

> Now you can practice any place, any time. Answer a question a day on the Daily Practice for the New SAT app and get immediate feedback. Available through the App Store and Google Play.

Show up ready on test day

Using Official SAT Practice will help you get familiar with the types of questions you'll see on the SAT and build your skills so you feel confident on test day.

A commitment to equity

The College Board is collaborating with teachers and community-based organizations such as the Boys & Girls Clubs of America to ensure that as many students as possible can take advantage of these resources. You can access these world-class online practice tools anytime from your local library, YMCA, or any other source with internet access. Just go to satpractice.org.

Multiple-Choice Strategies

Pay close attention to directions

Listen carefully to any instructions given by the test administrator and carefully read all directions in your booklet before you begin to answer the questions.

Know how to fill out the answer sheet

It is very important that you fill in the entire circle darkly and completely. If you change your answer, erase it as completely as possible. Incomplete marks or erasures may affect your score.

Don't lose your place

Check your answer sheet as you go along to make sure you are answering the right question in the right place.

Keep track of time

Don't spend too much time on any group of questions within a section.

Read the entire question, including all the answer choices, before answering a question

Don't think that because the first or second answer choice looks good to you, it isn't necessary to read the remaining options.

Watch out for absolutes

When a question or answer option contains words such as "always," "every," "only," "never," and "none," there can be no exceptions to the answer you choose. Use of words such as "often," "rarely," "sometimes," and "generally" indicates that there may be some exceptions to the answer.

Answer easy questions first

These are usually at the start of each section, and the harder ones are at the end. The exception is in the SAT's evidence-based reading and writing section, where questions are ordered according to the logic and organization of each passage.

Make educated guesses

On the redesigned SAT there are no deductions for wrong answers; only correct answers are scored. This "rights-only" scoring is meant to encourage students to give their best shot to every problem, without risking a penalty for trying their best. Since an educated guess can only work in your favor, try to rule out one or more answer choices, and you'll have a better chance of choosing the right answer.

Limit your time on any one question

All questions are worth the same number of points. If you need a lot of time to answer a question, go on to the next one. Later, you may have time to return to the question you skipped.

Mark the questions in your booklet that you skipped

That will save time if you want to go back and give these questions another try.

More Practice Tips

You won't need these tips to get ready for the SAT, because a complete, personalized practice program is available to you (see "Practice for Free" on page 105). But some colleges use other types of entrance and/or placement exams for admission, or for selective programs (like nursing), or to place students into the right courses. If such exams are part of the admission requirements at the colleges you are considering, the following tips provide a good plan of attack.

Look at sample tests

They are usually available for free at the testing organization's website. You'll be more confident if you know what to expect. Being familiar with the different sections will also save you valuable time during the test.

Next, take a practice exam

Do this to get a "starting score" so you can measure improvement. This will also enable you to see what types of questions you do well on, and what types you don't. Now you know what to concentrate on.

Look at your patterns and pacing

As you score your practice work, pay attention to the kinds of questions that give you trouble and focus your preparation accordingly. How was your pacing? If you finished early and got easy questions wrong, slow down and read questions more thoroughly.

Take advantage of "down" time

Drilling and subject matter review work best in short spurts over a longer period of time. Use down time—like when you're on a bus or in a waiting room—to do math drills, or read an outline. It'll sink in without wearing you out.

Take another practice test

Use the scores from this one to see how you've improved after studying. If you're not making headway, don't keep it to yourself—ask for help.

Take a final, timed test

Do this about a week before the exam. Don't cheat—use a timer and tell yourself "pencils down" when it goes off. The result will give you a good sense of how you'll do on the real thing.

Don't spend a lot of money

Self-discipline is free. Most expensive review courses just provide a dedicated place and time for you to do things you can do on your own.

Relax

College entrance exams are important, but they will NOT determine your future. They are just one part of your college application process. Just do your best, think positively, and you'll do fine.

Tips for Taking the SAT Subject Tests™

The SAT Subject Tests are used by colleges that want an objective way to evaluate what students know and can do in particular subject areas. Think of them as a chance to shine in subjects where you are strong.

If you are thinking of applying to colleges that require or recommend SAT Subject Tests, consider these test-taking tips.

Know when to take the Subject Tests

Take them when the content is fresh in your mind—often at the end of the course for subjects like biology, chemistry, and world history.

Know what to expect

Become familiar with the test format, the types of questions, and test-day procedures. Download *The SAT Subject Tests Student Guide* from www.collegeboard.org (or get a free copy from your counselor's office).

Know the test directions

For every five minutes you spend reading directions, you will have five fewer minutes available to answer questions. Learn the directions now.

Become familiar with the SAT Subject Test answer sheet

A copy appears in the back of *The Official Study Guide for all SAT Subject Tests™*. Your school library should have a copy of this publication.

Do the easier questions first

The easier questions are usually at the beginning of a grouping of questions. You can earn as many points for easy questions as you can for hard questions.

Don't be alarmed if you can't answer all the questions

Each Subject Test is designed to cover a wide range of knowledge, skills, and subject matter. Students are not expected to know and recognize everything covered in these tests. Typically, students answer only about half the questions correctly.

Know how the tests are scored

You get one point for each right answer and lose a fraction of a point for each wrong answer. You neither gain nor lose points for omitting an answer.

Make a smart guess

If you can rule out one or more answer choices for a multiple-choice question as definitely wrong, your chances of guessing correctly among the remaining choices improve. If you have no clue as to the correct answer, random guessing is not to your advantage. You should omit questions only when you really have no idea how to answer them.

Use the test book for scratch work

In your test book (but not on the answer sheet), cross off answers you know are wrong, and mark questions you did not answer so you can go back to them if you have time. Be sure to mark your answers on the separate answer sheet because you won't receive credit for any answers you marked in the test book.

Don't make extra marks on the answer sheet

The answer sheet is machine scored, and the machine can't tell an answer from a doodle.

Bring an acceptable calculator for the Mathematics Level 1 or Mathematics Level 2 tests

Acceptable means: graphing, scientific, or 4-function (not recommended). No laptops or other portable/handheld computers, or machines with typewriter-like keypads or paper tapes. Make sure you have fresh batteries.

Take an acceptable CD player for Language tests with listening

If you are taking any of the listening tests, you'll need your own CD player. (A list of what's acceptable can be found at satsubjecttests. org.) Be sure to also bring extra batteries. Test centers do not provide players or batteries, and you won't be allowed to share during the exam.

Need to decide whether to take Biology E or Biology M?

Look at the sample questions in the SAT Subject Test Practice section on satsubjecttests. org to see whether you are more comfortable with the ecological emphasis of Biology E or the molecular emphasis of Biology M. You should also consult with your biology teacher.

Need to decide whether to take Mathematics Level 1 or Mathematics Level 2?

Math Level 1 is designed for students who have taken two years of algebra and one year of geometry. Math Level 2 is designed for students who have taken an additional year covering elementary functions (precalculus) and/or trigonometry. If you have had preparation in trigonometry and elementary functions, have grades of B or better in these courses, and know when and how to use a scientific or graphing calculator, take Math Level 2.

Need to decide whether to take a Language Subject Test as a reading test or a listening test?

There is no difference in difficulty between these two types of language tests. However, the tests with listening can provide a more complete picture of your skills. For this reason, colleges may prefer the listening test to the reading-only test for placement purposes. If you are taking the test for admission purposes, college deadlines for submitting applications may determine the choice of test for you.

Plan your test-taking day

Think about these options and conditions:

- You can take up to three Subject Tests on one test date (but only one can be a listening test).

- You can change your mind on test day about which Subject Test you want to take.

- Except for listening tests, you may add a test or substitute a test on test day.

- You may work on only one test during each testing hour. (There are short breaks after each hour.)

SAT Test Day Tips/ What to Bring

No matter how many times you've been told to relax and not worry about it, on test day you'll likely be a bit nervous. Actually, a little tension is good—it will keep you sharp. But too much tension can hurt your performance. Here are some tips to help you arrive at the test center in good shape and ready to do your best.

Listen to Mom

- Get a good night's sleep before the exam.
- Set out your photo ID, admission ticket, the No. 2 pencils you'll need, and fresh erasers before bed, to avoid last-minute nuttiness in the morning.
- Eat breakfast. You'll be at the test center for several hours and you're likely to get hungry.

Know how you'll get to the test location

If you've been assigned to a test site you're unfamiliar with (that can happen, especially if you register late), make sure you print out and review directions, and leave enough time for unexpected delays.

Leave early enough so you won't have to rush or be late

You don't need the extra anxiety. Plan to arrive at the test center by 7:45 a.m. Testing starts at about 8 a.m.

If you didn't register in time

If you miss the late registration deadline, there's still a chance that you can take the SAT. Test centers accept standbys on a first-come, first-served basis only if the site has enough space, testing materials, and staff—so there is no guarantee that you'll be admitted to the test.

What you really need to bring:

- You MUST bring acceptable Photo ID and your SAT Admission Ticket. You won't be allowed in otherwise. Acceptable ID means: current; government- or school-issued; with a recent, recognizable photo; and bearing your name in English (matching the name on your admission ticket). Visit sat.org/test-day for the latest information and to review the complete Photo ID policy.
- Be sure to bring two No. 2 pencils and a good, soft eraser. It must be a No. 2 in order to be machine-readable. (It's the most common type of pencil so this should not be a problem.) Mechanical pencils and pens are not allowed, even for the essay. And check that the eraser erases cleanly, without smudges.

It's also a good idea to bring:

- An acceptable calculator with fresh batteries. Acceptable means: battery-operated, graphing, scientific, or 4-function. No laptops or other portable/handheld computers, smart phones, tablets, or other devices with typewriter-like keypads or paper tapes are permitted.

- Snacks. You will get several short breaks, and you can eat or drink any snacks you have brought with you during these breaks. A healthy snack will go a long way toward keeping you alert during the entire test.

- A watch (but no audible alarm please) to pace yourself.

- A backpack or bag to keep your stuff under your seat.

What not to bring:

- Cell phone, pager, personal digital assistant, iPod, MP3 player, BlackBerry, or other digital/electronic equipment.

- Scratch paper.

- Notes, books, dictionary.

- Compass, protractor, ruler, or any other aid.

- Highlighter or colored pencils.

- Portable listening or recording device (unless you're taking a SAT Subject Test with a listening component).

- Camera or other photographic equipment.

- Timer with audible alarm.

Calculator tips:

- Bring a calculator with you. Calculators will not be given out at the test center.

- If you don't use a calculator regularly, practice using it before the test. Bring a calculator you're familiar with.

- Don't buy an expensive, sophisticated calculator just to take the test.

- You don't have to use a calculator on every question in the calculator section. First, decide how to solve the problem, and then decide whether to use the calculator. The calculator should help you, not get in the way.

- It may help to do scratch work in the test book. Get your thoughts down before using your calculator.

- Make sure your calculator is in good working order and that batteries are fresh. If your calculator fails during testing and you have no backup, you'll have to complete the test without it.

If You Need Accommodations

If you have a documented disability, you may be eligible for appropriate accommodations to enable you to take a test. The information given here applies to all College Board tests, such as the PSAT/NMSQT, SAT, SAT Subject Tests, or AP Exams. To find out about similar policies for other exams, visit the testing organization's website.

Types of accommodations available

The College Board's procedures for determining appropriate accommodations on its tests provide for considerable flexibility to accommodate your special needs. There are four major categories for testing accommodations:

Presentation (e.g., large print; reader; Braille; Braille device for written responses; visual magnification; auditory amplification; MP3 audio; sign/oral presentations);

Responding (e.g., verbal/dictated to scribe; tape recorder; computer without spell check/grammar/cut & paste features; large block answer sheet);

Timing/scheduling (e.g., frequent breaks; extended time; multiple day; specified time of day); and

Setting (e.g., small group setting; private room; special lighting/acoustics; adaptive/special furniture/tools; alternative test site [with proctor present]; preferential seating).

How to apply for accommodations

You can apply through your school. This is how most students apply for accommodations. You or your parents must first complete a consent form, and then your school's SSD Coordinator will be able to request accommodations through SSD Online.

Or you can apply directly yourself. You or your parents can request accommodations without the assistance of a school, by submitting a Student Eligibility Form directly to the College Board (available by contacting the College Board Services for Students with Disabilities).

> For a more complete discussion of all you should know, go to the "Services for Students with Disabilities" section on **collegeboard.org**.

What about documentation? In some cases, documentation will be requested for the College Board's review. If you apply through your school, SSD Online will indicate if documentation is required. If you choose to apply directly without going through your school, documentation is always required. Guidelines for documentation are available on collegeboard.org.

Start the process early. It can take up to seven weeks to review the application after it's completed, so you should begin the process at least three months before the test date.

After Approval

You and your school will receive an Eligibility Letter notifying you of the approved accommodations. The letters will include an SSD Eligibility Code for you.

If you are taking the SAT, be sure to provide your SSD Eligibility Code when you register, and bring your eligibility letter to the test with you.

If you are taking an AP Exam or the PSAT/NMSQT, be sure to inform your school that you have been approved for accommodations, so that they may make arrangements and order appropriate materials.

> If you receive **approval just before the test**, contact the College Board to make sure the accommodations will be available on the test date.

If you transfer to a new school, inform your new school that you were approved for accommodations, and give the school your SSD Eligibility Code.

Eligibility requirements

Basic requirements for eligibility include the following:

1. You must have a documented disability.
2. The disability must impact your ability to participate in standardized tests.
3. You must demonstrate a need for the specific accommodation requested. (For example, if you ask for extended time, you must show that your disability causes difficulty with test taking under timed conditions.)

Note that the use of accommodations in school, or inclusion on an Individual Education Program (IEP) or 504 Plan, does not automatically qualify you for accommodations on College Board tests.

If you have a temporary disability

If you have a temporary disability, such as a broken arm, you should register for a test on a later date when the temporary disability has healed. This is the process for the SAT tests that are administered throughout the academic year. However, if you are planning to take a test that is only administered annually (e.g., AP Exams or the PSAT/NMSQT), you or your school may contact the College Board to inquire if it would be possible for you to test with temporary accommodations.

Test-Taking Timeline

This timeline covers all SAT, SAT Subject Tests, and AP Exams. Use it to scope out all the upcoming dates and deadlines for the tests you'll be taking. *Be sure to check the specific test dates and registration deadlines for the year you are taking the tests*—they change slightly year to year. You'll find them on collegeboard.org.

Junior Year

SEPTEMBER

Pick up the *PSAT/NMSQT Student Guide* from your guidance office and take the practice test.

OCTOBER

The **PSAT/NMSQT** is administered this month.

DECEMBER

- Register for the **SAT** by the end of this month, if you want to take it in **March**. (No SAT Subject Tests are administered in March.)
- Begin preparing for the SAT for free. Go to **satpractice.org**.

JANUARY

Review your PSAT/NMSQT **Score Report** with your school counselor. Talk about what courses to take next year, based on your results.

FEBRUARY

- If you're taking AP classes, **register for AP Exams**, given in May.
- If you're not in an AP course but want to take an AP Exam, contact AP Services for a list of local AP Coordinators by the end of this month.

MARCH

- The **SAT** is administered this month, but not SAT Subject Tests.
- If you're not in an AP course but want to take an AP Exam, you must make final arrangements to take AP Exams by **March 15**.
- Register for the **SAT** and **SAT Subject Tests** by the end of this month, if you want to take them in **May**.

APRIL

Register for the **SAT** and **SAT Subject Tests** by the end of this month, if you want to take them in **June**.

MAY

- **AP Exams** are given this month.
- The **SAT** and **SAT Subject Tests** are administered this month.
- Register for the **SAT** and **SAT Subject Tests** by the end of this month, if you want to take them in **August**.

JUNE

- The **SAT** and **SAT Subject Tests** are administered this month.

AUGUST

- The **SAT** and **SAT Subject Tests** are administered this month.

Senior Year

SEPTEMBER

- Register for the **SAT** and **SAT Subject Tests** by the beginning of this month, if you want to take them in **October**.
- Register for the **SAT** and **SAT Subject Tests** before the end of this month, if you want to take them in **November. NOTE: November is the only month you can take Language Tests with Listening.**

OCTOBER

- The **SAT** and **SAT Subject Tests** are administered this month.
- Register for the **SAT** and **SAT Subject Tests** by the end of this month, if you want to take them in **December**.

NOVEMBER

- The **SAT** and **SAT Subject Tests** are administered this month.

DECEMBER

- The **SAT** and **SAT Subject Tests** are administered this month.
- Register for **SAT** and **SAT Subject Tests** before the end of this month, if you want to take them in **January**.

JANUARY

- The **SAT** and **SAT Subject Tests** are administered this month.
- Register for the **SAT** by the end of this month, if you want to take it in **March**. (No SAT Subject Tests are administered in March.)

FEBRUARY

- If you're taking AP classes, **register for AP Exams**, given in May.
- If you're not in an AP course but want to take an AP Exam, contact AP Services for a list of local AP Coordinators by the end of this month.

MARCH

- The **SAT** is administered this month, but not SAT Subject Tests.
- If you're not in an AP course but want to take an AP Exam, you must make final arrangements to take AP Exams by **March 15**.
- Register for the **SAT** and **SAT Subject Tests** by the end of this month, if you want to take them in **May**.

APRIL

Register for the **SAT** and **SAT Subject Tests** by the end of this month, if you want to take them in **June**.

MAY

- **AP Exams** are given this month.
- The **SAT** and **SAT Subject Tests** are administered this month.

JUNE

- The **SAT** and **SAT Subject Tests** are administered this month.

Test-Taking Tracker

This tracker will help you stay on top of all the college admission tests you might need to take. Use it together with the "College Application Tracker" on page 126.

Put in the names of the colleges you are applying to, the dates for all reminders and deadlines, and check off when done.

		SAT	ACT
REQUIRED OR RECOMMENDED	College 1		
	College 2		
	College 3		
	College 4		
	College 5		
	College 6		
	College 7		
	College 8		
REGISTRATION	Registration deadline (for test in the fall)		
	Registration deadline (for test in the winter)		
	Registration deadline (for test in the spring)		
	Registration fee		
DATE TEST TAKEN	Fall test date		
	Winter test date		
	Spring test date		
SCORES	Score received		
	Request scores be sent to colleges		
	Score sent		

SAT SUBJECT TEST	SAT SUBJECT TEST	AP EXAM	AP EXAM

Completing
the Applications

Application Basics

Here's a quick rundown of what to expect as you start filling out college applications, and what you need to do to get them done.

Keeping on track

The first thing you should do is write down the application deadlines and all the tasks you'll have to accomplish to complete the applications. (See the "College Application Tracker" on page 126.)

Most applications for regular admission are due in early January or February, and most early application deadlines are in November or December. So try to lay out your timeline in October of your senior year. (My Organizer on collegeboard.org will help you plan and remind you of upcoming deadlines.)

Remember to budget time for other people to do things. Teachers won't write recommendations overnight, and testing organizations will need a few weeks to send official score reports to colleges.

> Most colleges have two separate application forms: one for admission, and one for financial aid. The deadlines for these forms may be different as well.

Filling out the application

A typical application will ask you to provide some personal information; what schools you have attended; brief descriptions of your extracurricular activities, jobs, and any academic honors you have earned; and standardized test scores. They will also ask for information about your family and their education background, to see if you merit special consideration as a first-generation college student, or if you are related to an alumnus.

Finally, all applications will ask if you plan to file for financial aid. Checking this box does not mean you have applied for financial aid! It just lets the admission office know that they should coordinate with the financial aid office later on. You'll have to file for financial aid separately.

What goes with your application

Besides the application form, there are several things that need to be included with your application. You will have to send some of them with the form; others will be sent to the college by other people.

Application fee—usually nonrefundable. Many colleges offer fee waivers for applicants from low-income families, and some waive the fee if you apply online.

High school transcript—Your high school should send your transcript, along with a school profile, directly to the colleges you are applying to.

Admission test scores—if the college requires standardized test scores, you must make sure the testing agency itself sends an official score report. You can't write them down yourself or send a photocopy.

Letters of recommendation—if required, they are usually sent directly to the college by the person writing the letter; but sometimes your school counselor will assemble the letters and send them with your transcript. (See "Guidelines for Getting Recommendations" on page 132.)

If you apply online, remember to print them out and proofread them before you submit the application, just as you would with a printed application. Also, be sure to inform your school counselor that you've applied online—your school will need to send your transcript to the college.

Essays or personal statements—most colleges don't require these, but selective ones do. Some applications will ask you to attach a separate essay of one or two pages, others will ask you to fill in some one-paragraph short responses directly on the application form, and others will ask for both. See Chapter 8 for lots of tips about essays.

Auditions, portfolios, and other supplementary materials—if you're applying for a performing or fine arts program, you may have to demonstrate your ability by auditioning on campus or submitting an audiotape, slides, or some other sample of your work. Talk to a teacher or mentor in your subject for advice on both how to assemble a portfolio and which of your pieces to include. Be sure to check the deadlines for auditions—they are often different from the deadlines for applications.

Take your time

College applications aren't difficult, but they are important. Admission committees will take a sloppy or careless submission as a reflection on you. So take the time to do a careful, neat job. Review each section and proofread your answers. This is equally true of online applications. (See "Online Application Dos and Don'ts" on page 129.)

College Application Timeline

College applications won't seem so overwhelming if you know what's coming, and what needs to be done when. Use this timeline to get a bird's-eye view of the whole process. This is only a general guide and may not apply to all colleges, so check the specific requirements and deadlines of the colleges you are applying to.

SUMMER BEFORE SENIOR YEAR

- **Create your list of colleges** that really interest you. Match them up against your list of "must haves" and "like to haves." (See the "What You Want Checklist" on page 78.)

- **Visit** some colleges on your list. Call ahead for the campus tour schedule.

- Register for the SAT and/or SAT Subjects Tests if you intend to take them in the fall.

- If you plan on competing in Division I or Division II **college sports**, register with the NCAA Eligibility Center.

- Find out about **local scholarships** offered by church groups, civic associations, and businesses in your area.

SEPTEMBER

- Meet with your school counselor to **finalize your list of colleges**. Be sure your list includes "safety," "probable," and "reach" schools. (See "Your Short List of Colleges" on page 80.)

- Get an **FSA ID** for both yourself and one of your parents from www.fafsa.ed.gov. You'll need them for the FAFSA financial aid form.

- If you are going to apply under an **Early Decision or Early Action plan**, get started now. Deadlines for early applications tend to fall in October or November.

- Set up campus visits and interviews and attend **open houses** at colleges on your list.

OCTOBER

- Register for the SAT and/or SAT Subject Tests if you want to take them in December or January.

- Ask for **letters of recommendation** from your counselor, teachers, coaches, or employers.

- **Start working on your FAFSA** and submit it as soon as you can after Oct. 1. Go to **www.fafsa.ed.gov** to access the form.

- Write **first drafts of your college essays** and ask your parents and teachers to review them.

NOVEMBER

- Submit **Early Decision and Early Action** applications on time. Save a copy for yourself and your school counselor.

- Finish your application **essays**. Proofread them rigorously for mistakes.

- Apply to colleges with rolling admission (first-come, first-served) as early as possible.

- Give your school counselor the proper forms to **send transcripts** to your colleges at least two weeks in advance.

- Follow up on your letters of recommendation to be sure they go out on time.

DECEMBER

- Try to **wrap up college applications** before winter break. Make copies for yourself and your school counselor.

- If you applied for early decision, you should have an answer by Dec. 15. If you are denied or deferred, submit applications now to other colleges.

- Contact the financial aid office at the colleges on your list to make sure you have all required **financial aid forms**.

JANUARY

- Submit your **FAFSA** as soon as you can if you haven't already. Check your college's financial aid deadlines and priority dates; some can be as early as Feb. 1.

- Submit other financial aid forms that may be required—such as the CSS Profile or the college's own forms. Keep copies.

- If a college wants to see your **midyear grades**, tell your school counselor.

- If you have acquired any new honors or accomplishments, let your colleges know.

FEBRUARY

- Contact your colleges to confirm that all application materials have been received.

- If any special circumstances affect your family's financial situation, alert each college's financial aid office.

MARCH

- Admission decisions start arriving. Read everything you receive carefully, as some may require prompt action on your part.

- **Revisit colleges** that accepted you if it's hard to make a choice.

- Don't get senioritis! Colleges want to see strong second half grades.

APRIL

- Most admission decisions and financial aid award letters arrive this month. Carefully **compare financial aid** award letters from the colleges that accept you.

- Make a final decision, accept the aid package and **mail a deposit check** to the college you select before May 1 (the acceptance deadline for most schools).

- Notify the other colleges that you won't be attending (so another student can have your spot).

- On the waiting list? Contact the admission office and let them know of your continued interest in the college and update them on your spring semester grades and activities.

MAY

- AP Exams are given. Make sure your AP Grade Report is sent to your college.

- Finalize your **housing** plans if you're living away. Send in all required forms and deposits.

- Study hard for final exams. Most admission offers are contingent on your final grades.

- **Thank everyone** who wrote you recommendations or otherwise helped with your college applications.

JUNE

- Have your counselor send your **final transcript** to your college choice.

- If you plan on competing in Division I or Division II college sports, have your counselor send your final transcript to the NCAA Eligibility Center.

- Enjoy your graduation, and **have a great summer!**

College Application Tracker

This tracker will help you stay on top of all your application tasks, paperwork, and deadlines. Put in all due dates, and check them off when done. Use it together with the "Financial Aid Application Tracker" on page 170.

		COLLEGE 1	COLLEGE 2
Deadlines	Regular application deadline (check fin aid deadlines)		
	Early application deadline		
Grades	High school transcript sent		
	Midyear grade reports sent		
Test Scores	SAT or ACT required?		
	SAT Subject Tests required?		
	Release SAT Subject Test scores		
	Send SAT scores		
	Send ACT scores		
	Send AP grades		
Letters of Recommendation	Number required		
	Request teacher recommendations		
	Request counselor recommendation		
	Request other recommendations		
	Send thank-you notes		
Essays	Essay required?		
	Proof for spelling and grammar		
	Have two people read your essay		
	Final copy in application		
Interviews	Interview required?		
	Interview date		
	Send thank-you notes to interviewers		
Submitting the Application	Sign application and keep a copy of everything		
	Pay application fee (amount)		
	Applied online—received confirmation receipt		
	Applied by mail—confirm receipt of all materials		
	Notified school counselor that you applied		
	Send supplemental material, if needed		
After You Send Your Application	Received decision letter from office of admission		
	Deadline to accept admission and send deposit		
	Tuition deposit sent		
	Housing forms completed and deposit sent		
	Notify the other colleges you will not attend		

COLLEGE 3	COLLEGE 4	COLLEGE 5	COLLEGE 6	COLLEGE 7	COLLEGE 8
SCHOOL NAME	SCHOOL NAME	SCHOOL NAME	SCHOOL NAME	SCHOOL NAME	SCHOOL NAME

College Application FAQs

Do I have a better chance of getting in if I apply early decision?

The answer varies from college to college and year to year, but in general, applying early decision gives you somewhat better odds of acceptance. But don't apply early decision just because you think it will give you a competitive advantage. You should go that route only if you are absolutely sure you want to attend that college more than any other. For more advice, see "What to Know About Applying Early" on page 131.

What is the Common Application? Should I use it?

The Common Application is an online form used by over 500 colleges and universities that belong to the Common Application Group. They all agree to accept this application in place of their own (although some require an additional supplement). You fill it out once and it is then transmitted to all of your colleges that participate. To learn more, see "About the Common Application" on page 130, or go to www.commonapp.org.

My SAT scores are very low, and my grades are very high. Will this affect my chances of admission?

While SAT scores are an indicator of success in college, it's only one of many different factors colleges will look at while evaluating your application. The main thing they look for is to see if your high school record indicates that you have the potential for academic success on their campus. If you've done well in challenging courses in high school, that usually is given greater weight than test scores.

My parents don't make a lot of money—will colleges hold this against me?

Some colleges declare that they have a "need-blind" admission policy. That means they never consider ability to pay as an admission criterion. Other schools, which are "need-conscious," may consider ability to pay, but only for a very small portion of applicants. The advice of most counselors: Don't worry about this.

Is it okay to send additional material that I think will support my application?

It is okay to provide additional information to explain something that cannot be explained on the application forms, but other items that students sometimes send are not helpful and may be viewed as trying to distract the admission staff from the actual application. Talk to your school counselor about any additional items that you are thinking about sending.

Do colleges really care about your senior year grades?

Absolutely! Many colleges will not make a decision until receiving midyear senior grades. Colleges also ask for a final transcript at the end of the senior year. (Admission letters often contain something like, "Your admission is contingent upon your continued successful performance.") It is not at all rare for a college to withdraw an offer of admission when grades drop significantly over the course of the senior year.

Online Application Dos and Don'ts

Applying online is fast, easy, always neat and clean, and often free. But it's not all good—there are some pitfalls for the unwary. Here are the key dos and don'ts.

Do:

create user names, PIN numbers, and passwords that you'll remember easily. Write them down and keep them in a safe place.

Don't:

treat an online application casually—it's an important document that reflects on you. don't use abbreviations and short spellings as if you were texting.

Don't:

be too quick to click. Take your time, follow all directions, and complete each step with care. Scroll each page from top to bottom and read every pop-up, to be sure you don't miss any information.

Don't:

forget to periodically save your work. You might get "timed out" if you don't enter anything for a while (usually 30 minutes). If you need to take a break, use the save/log-out feature to store your application, then log back in.

Don't:

compose your essay or personal statement in the space allotted online. Draft (and re-draft) these separately in a word-processing application, such as Microsoft® Word, then copy and paste the final draft into the online application.

Do:

print and save a hard copy of the completed application. Proofread it before you hit the "send" button—sometimes your information in text boxes can get cut off.

Do:

ask someone else to review the application for errors before you send it. Two sets of eyes are always better than one.

Do:

print and save a copy of the confirmation page that should appear after you submit the application, so that you'll have a record of your application ID number.

Do:

tell your school counselor about every online application you submit. Better yet, give your counselor a hard copy printout. This is critical, because your application won't be complete until your counselor forwards your transcript and any other material the college may require.

Don't:

apply online and then send a paper copy in the mail. That will just confuse things.

Do:

call or e-mail the college if you haven't received an e-mail confirmation of receipt within 48 hours. Online submissions do get lost occasionally. (That's why it's so important to print and save.)

Don't:

apply online the week before the application deadline. Because of high volume, application websites tend to get slow and cranky at this time. It's also the most likely time for a system failure. If you're up against the deadline, it's safer to apply through the mail.

About the Common Application

Much of what goes into a typical college application is the same as what goes into any other: your name and address, your high school information, your extracurriculars, etc. If you're applying to several colleges it can be annoying—and time consuming—to rekey this same info over and over.

Fill it out once, submit it to multiple colleges

The Common Application is designed to relieve students of this repetitive process by providing a single application form (print and online) that is accepted by over 500 participating colleges. You fill it out once and then submit copies to any number of these institutions. The same is true of the school report and the teacher evaluation portions, which are automatically submitted with the application.

There might be an additional step

Member colleges of the Common Application Group make no distinction between the common application and their own form when making admission decisions. However, some member colleges require supplemental forms in addition to the common application. You should research whether the colleges to which you are applying need such a form by consulting their websites.

Transfer students can use it too

There's a Common Application for students who are applying for transfer admission as well as first-year admission. The Transfer Application is designed primarily for online submission, but you can download a printable PDF form if need be.

To access the Common Application and to find out which colleges participate, go to **www.commonapp.org**.

Not all colleges use it

Membership in the Common Application Group is restricted to colleges that use a holistic selection process to evaluate applicants. That means they use subjective as well as objective criteria, such as recommendations, an essay, and other considerations beyond grades and test scores. Sending the Common Application to nonmembers is discouraged.

Don't forget your counselor

The Common Application can be a great time-saver—but remember to inform your school counselor of every college you send it to.

What to Know About Applying Early

If you find a college that you're sure is right for you, consider applying early. Early Decision and Early Action plans allow you to apply early (usually in November) and get an admission decision early (usually by Dec. 15).

Early Decision plans are binding

You agree to attend the college if it accepts you and offers an adequate financial aid package. You can apply to only one college for Early Decision. You may also apply to other colleges through the regular admission process, but if you're accepted by your first-choice college early, you must withdraw all other applications.

Early Action plans are nonbinding

While the college will tell you whether or not you're accepted by early January, you have the right to wait until May 1 before responding. This gives you time to compare colleges, including their financial aid offers, before making a decision. You can also apply Early Action to more than one college.

> Get advice from your school counselor before applying Early Decision. While it may seem appealing to get the process over with early, it might be too soon to know that you've made the right college choice.

Single-choice Early Action is another option offered by a few colleges

This plan works the same way as other Early Action plans, but candidates may not apply early (either Early Action or Early Decision) to any other school. You can still apply for regular admission to other schools and are not required to give your final answer of acceptance until the regular decision deadline.

If you need financial aid, Early Decision might not be a good idea

You shouldn't apply under an Early Decision plan if you think you'll be better off weighing financial aid packages from several colleges later in the spring. While you can turn down an early acceptance if the college is unable to meet your need for financial aid, "need" in this context is determined by formulas, not by your family.

Not every college offers an early plan

More than 400 colleges offer an Early Decision plan, an Early Action plan, or both; but that is only about 20 percent of all four-year colleges.

Guidelines for Getting Recommendations

Most colleges want two or three recommendation letters from people who know you in and out of the classroom. Often they require at least one from an academic teacher (sometimes for a specific subject), and/or your school counselor. Here are some tips on whom—and how—to ask.

The best teacher to ask is...

If you don't have a clear favorite, your English or math teachers usually make good candidates. Ask a teacher from junior year unless a current teacher has known you long enough to form an opinion.

Think about which teacher will remember you best, because of your class participation and any personal interaction. That may be a teacher in whose class you've gotten top grades, but it could also be a teacher who knows how hard you've worked to get B's and C's.

The best time to ask is...

Ask at least one month ahead of your deadline, two weeks at a minimum. If you're asking a popular teacher, he or she might have a lot of letters to write. And be sure to also allow time for snail mail. Often the college's deadline is receipt date, not the postmark date.

The best way to ask is...

Remember you're asking for a favor; don't demand one.

Don't be shy. Teachers and counselors are usually happy to help you, as long as you respect their time constraints.

Ask in a way that allows a teacher to decline comfortably if he/she does not have time to do an adequate job. For example: "Do you feel you know me well enough, and do you have enough time to write a letter of recommendation for me?"

Follow up with a written request with instructions, the deadline, and an addressed and stamped envelope. (See the "Sample Recommendation Request Letter" on the next page.)

Give them something to work with

Provide a "brag sheet" or résumé reminding them of your accomplishments over the years. (See the "Recommendation Cheat Sheet" on page 134.) It will make their job easier.

Follow up

Follow up with your recommendation writers a week or so prior to your first deadline, to ensure recommendations have been mailed or to see if they need additional information from you. And send a thank-you note to everyone who provided a recommendation.

Sample Recommendation Request Letter

This letter can be short and sweet, but what's most important is not to wait until the last minute. Give the person you're asking enough time to write the recommendation and send it off ahead of any deadlines. A month is best; the **minimum** is two weeks.

Your Name
Street Address
City, State, Zip

October _ _, 20_ _

[*Name of person you are asking*]
Street Address
City, State, Zip

Dear _____,
I am applying for admission to [*name of college(s)*], and I need a letter of recommendation.

Would you consider writing a letter for me? I have attached the instructions for the letter, and an addressed and stamped envelope for each school. I have also attached a short résumé of my accomplishments, which I hope you find helpful.

My deadline for recommendations is _____, 20__.

Thank you so much. I really appreciate your taking time to do this for me.

Sincerely,

Recommendation Cheat Sheet

Here's a "cheat sheet" that will make the job easier for those who are writing your recommendations. The more details about your background you can give, the more thorough their recommendation will be. This worksheet will also help you with the entire college application process, especially in preparing for interviews and writing admission essays. (Have you kept up an "Extracurricular Archive" like the one on page 35?)

Name: _____

Date: _____

SCHOOL ACTIVITIES

List the activities you have participated in, the number of years, and the amount of time per week you spent. Write a sentence or two stating what you have gained or learned from each activity. Mention any leadership positions held, or specific contributions you made. For sports, mention any highlights that you are most proud of.

ACTIVITY: _____ YEARS: _____ HOURS/WEEK: _____

_____

_____

_____

ACTIVITY: _____ YEARS: _____ HOURS/WEEK: _____

_____

_____

_____

ACTIVITY: _____ YEARS: _____ HOURS/WEEK: _____

_____

_____

_____

_____

WHICH ACTIVITY WAS MOST IMPORTANT TO YOU? WHY?

OUTSIDE ACTIVITIES

What do you consider your most important activities outside of school? List jobs (paid or unpaid); community service; religious activities; hobbies; travel; music, art, or drama. Include the number of years of your involvement and the amount of time you spent on the activity weekly.

ACTIVITY: YEARS: HOURS/WEEK:

ACTIVITY: YEARS: HOURS/WEEK:

ACTIVITY: YEARS: HOURS/WEEK:

WHICH ACTIVITY WAS MOST IMPORTANT TO YOU? WHY?

CONTINUED

HONORS AND AWARDS
In or out of school, which awards and honors have you received?

_____

_____

_____

_____

_____

ACADEMIC PROFILE
Describe the academic accomplishment (research paper, science experiment, artistic project) you are most proud of, and tell why you take pride in it.

_____

_____

_____

_____

_____

What kind of learner are you? Which academic setting or assignments make you thrive? What interests you?

_____

_____

_____

_____

_____

PERSONAL PROFILE
List your most distinguishing or most admirable qualities. Explain each in several sentences.

_____

_____

_____

_____

_____

_____

What book(s) have had the greatest impact on you? Why?

Title: _____   Author: _____

_____

_____

_____

Title: _____   Author: _____

_____

_____

_____

Title: _____   Author: _____

_____

_____

_____

WHAT DO YOU HOPE TO ACCOMPLISH IN COLLEGE AND AFTER?
Consider your career goals and your broader goals.

_____

_____

_____

_____

_____

_____

_____

_____

Source: Lick-Wilmerding High School, California

Art Portfolio Prep Tips

If you are applying to art school, your portfolio will be the most important part of your application. These tips will help you put together a great portfolio, no matter what kind of art you want to study.

Creating Your Portfolio

Know what each school wants to see

In general, an admissions portfolio consists of 10 to 15 images of your best and most recent work, but be sure to check each school's website for their specific requirements. Almost every school will want to see:

- **Observational drawings.** These are drawings from real life (never a photo), such as a landscape, room interior, portrait, or still life. Schools like them because they show your ability to interpret, compose, and accurately depict what you see before you.
- **Figure drawings.** The human figure drawn from life is one of the best things to include. A friend, yourself, someone in the park…
- **Variety.** Show you can work with different media (oil, watercolor, photography, clay, computer art, etc.), styles, and subjects.
- **Design skills.** Include a collage, poster, or layout that shows you can combine different elements.
- **That you've taken some risks.** Show that you are willing to challenge yourself.

But no school wants to see:

- Images of anime and video game imagery— it's so overdone
- Paintings or drawings copied from photos or other art works

Give yourself plenty of time

Get started early in your junior year. The more time you have to work, the more work you will have to choose from. An early start will also allow time for filling gaps and meeting specific school requirements.

Good quality work that really shows your strengths is hard to create when you are under time pressure. Besides, you should have some fun with this.

Be ready for inspiration

Always have a sketchbook, camera, or journal with you wherever you go. Everything around you is potential subject matter, so be ready to catch the moment.

Try to attend a summer or precollege program

These programs usually last four to six weeks, giving you the opportunity to not only build your portfolio but to get a sense of what art school is really like. They are also a lower-cost alternative to an expensive portfolio prep class. Ask your art teacher about any programs being offered at local colleges, art schools, or community centers.

Attend a National Portfolio Day

This is one of the best things you can do. National Portfolio Day events take place all over the country during the fall. It's sort of like a college fair for art schools, except the main focus is on evaluating portfolios brought in by students. Check it out at www.portfolioday.net

It's OK if the portfolio you bring is still a work in progress; in fact, it's to your advantage, since it allows you to incorporate the feedback you receive.

Don't do this alone

Get as much feedback as you can. Ask your teachers, family, friends, or other people whose opinions you trust to look at your work. Be open-minded about what you hear.

Submitting Your Portfolio

Don't leave this part to the last minute

Properly editing, photographing, documenting, and packaging your work for submission is painstaking work. Allow yourself several days to do it right. Plan to have all your works completed at least two weeks before the submission deadline.

Know the requirements

Every art program has its own rules about how it wants to receive works. So be sure to check each school's website for their submission guidelines and print them out. Pay special attention to the labeling and documentation requirements.

- **If submitting on a CD/DVD**, check for specs on dpi and pixel size. You'll also have to provide an inventory sheet with thumbnail images and descriptions of each piece.
- **If submitting slides**, allow time for developing, reviewing (you'll need a viewer) and labeling.
- **If submitting new media**, verify what format or software the school specifies or can accommodate.

Have someone help you photograph your work

It'll be easier with two people to handle the pieces and set up the shots. More photo tips:

- Use a good quality camera. (Don't use your phone.)
- Use a tripod to ensure consistent, well-centered shots.
- Shoot in daylight for best color and shadow control.

- Provide a solid white or black background, depending on the piece.
- Shoot three-dimensional works from different angles, and use light, shadow, and depth-of-field (short f-stop) to emphasize the piece.
- Keep a record of each shot, so you don't lose track.

Submit online if you can

Uploading your portfolio images to an online portfolio management website like SlideRoom is the easiest and least expensive way to submit your work. In fact, it's the preferred method at many major art schools.

You can post still and video works, edit and document them online, and after you click "submit" you'll get immediate confirmation that your work was received.

Keep a copy of everything you mail

You don't want to start over if any CD/DVDs or slides get lost or damaged. Also, mail your portfolio "return receipt requested," and follow up with each school to be sure everything arrived OK. Then reward yourself for a job well done!

TIPS

Tips for a Winning Music School Audition

If you want to pursue a degree in a music or performing arts program, an audition will probably be part of the application process. Here are some tips to help you do your best.

Before the Audition

Know what they want to hear

Each school is different so be sure to check the college website or contact the program directly for their audition guidelines. See if they require any specific works, styles, tempos, scales, or other technical demonstrations. Do this early enough to prepare and practice them.

Most schools will want you to:

- Demonstrate your best technical ability, but not perfection. (They expect you to be a student, not a pro.) Musical expressiveness, good intonation (define), and tonal quality usually counts more than technical virtuosity.
- Perform scales in a range of styles and speeds.
- Show you can sight read (playing or singing a piece of music while reading the notes for the first time).

Know what to expect

Ask the school about the audition's format: how long it should take, who will be there, what kind of room. Find out if it includes tests on theory or ear-training. Try to connect with a student who has gone through an audition at the same school recently. Your music teachers will have good insights too.

Select varied pieces

If allowed to choose, select different types of music that show your versatility, are expressive of your personality and showcase your strengths. Ask your teachers to help you select pieces that will impress, but are still within your skill level.

If it's a vocal audition, operas and show tunes are good sources. Pick two pieces in contrasting styles, and it would be good if one is in a foreign language.

Schedule early

Having a good pick of date and time is a stress reliever.

Give yourself lots of time to prepare

Don't even think you can cram for this, or that talent alone will see you through. You might be the best in your high school, but that's probably true of everyone else auditioning.

Practice the audition, not just the music

Perform your selected pieces in front of a variety of people and in different situations. Videotape these sessions and go over them with a teacher.

Be ready to talk, too

Many auditions are part interview as well. You might be asked about:

- Your teachers and other musicians who have influenced you.
- Your instrument—why you chose it, make and model, etc.
- Your repertoire—the composer, dates, genre, etc.
- Your own questions for them. (See Chapter 9.)

Take care of maintenance

Make sure your instrument is in good condition, and spiff it up a bit—appearance counts.

That goes for you too

Your physical condition affects your performance. Stay rested, eat well, exercise. Take care of yourself—plenty of rest, good nutrition, exercise, vitamins.

At the Audition

What to bring:

- Extra supplies, depending on your instrument.
- Your high school transcript and/or résumé.
- Copies of your music.
- If you're going to sing, try to bring an accompanist you are familiar with.

Arrive in good shape

Avoid caffeine the night before. Eat a light breakfast, but don't skip it. Drink water so you don't get dehydrated.

Look good

Your appearance is part of the performance. Dress well, but comfortably.

Arrive early

Give yourself extra time to find the audition room—it might be in an obscure place. Better yet, do a practice run if you can. Being late is the worst way to start.

Warm up

Another reason to arrive early. But don't overdo it or let it make you late.

If they cut you off

Don't be surprised or rattled if they tell you to stop in the middle of a piece—it's just a time-management thing.

If you have to sight-read

Check for the key, time signatures, and tempo before you begin.

Leave with a smile and a thank-you

Last impressions count too.

After the Audition

Send a thank-you note

You'd be surprised how important—and rare—this is. Send it to the head of the music department if you don't know a name.

If you really think you blew it

Ask for a second audition—some schools will accommodate such requests (but don't depend on it).

Keep perspective

It's not all about being judged—you are judging the school, too. Being accepted only matters if you will really be happy and successful there.

Home Schooled?

Most colleges are glad to admit home-schooled applicants, but the application process usually involves some additional steps to take and documentation to provide. If you are home schooled, review these tips so that you'll be ready to meet the extra requirements you'll face.

Make sure your home school curriculum covered college-prep material

There are certain "gatekeeper" courses that college admission officers expect all applicants to have completed. Your local school district or board of education should be able to verify that what you've studied is the equivalent of these college-preparatory classes.

Stay on top of dates and deadlines

Without regular announcements from a guidance office, it's up to you to keep track of critical dates and deadlines relating to things like college applications, test registration deadlines, or financial aid. You've already taken a good first step by buying this book!

Get recommendations

Many colleges require letters of recommendation. If your primary instructor is your parent, you might have to ask at least one unrelated adult who knows you well to write a letter. That could be a coach of a sports team, a leader of a club, or an employer—as long as the person has known you for a significant period of time and can speak about your character and abilities.

Search for home schooled–friendly colleges

Some colleges are friendlier toward home-schooled applicants than others. Before you select colleges, check to see if they have a home-school admission policy, or if they've admitted home-schoolers in the past. The best way to find out is to call admission offices directly and ask.

Prepare for a college interview

Interviews are often required or recommended for home-schooled applicants. Look upon this as an opportunity to present a more complete and accurate picture of yourself.

Know each college's application requirements

The requirements for home-schooled applicants can vary widely from college to college. Among the different requirements are:

- Transcript with course descriptions, syllabi, reading list, and grading criteria
- Portfolio of your work (such as research papers, projects, writing samples)
- State high school equivalency certificate, or other proof of district approval/accreditation
- Essay or personal statement
- GED
- SAT Subject Tests
- Statement describing home school structure and mission

Each home schooler's situation is different

For example, some students are associated with a particular home-based school program and others work with their local public school. The above tips speak generally about the college admission process for most home-schooled students. If you have any questions, contact your local high school's guidance office or call the admission office of the school to which you're applying.

No-Sweat
Application Essays

TIPS

Three Steps to a Great College Essay

The college application essay is a chance to reveal your personality, character, and spirit to the admission committee. Here's how to make the best of this chance—without making yourself crazy.

Remember—you already know how to write an essay

To write a college essay, use the exact same three-step process you'd use to write an essay for class: prewrite, draft, edit. This process will help you identify a focus for your essay, and gather the details you'll need to support it.

Step 1: Prewriting

To begin, first collect and organize potential ideas for your essay's focus.

Brainstorm

Make a list of your strengths and outstanding characteristics. Focus on strengths of personality, not things you've done. For example, you are responsible (not an "Eagle Scout") or committed (not "played basketball"). Use the "Topic Brainstorming Worksheet" on p. 148.

Discover your strengths

Do a little research about yourself: Ask parents, friends, and teachers what your strengths are.

Create a self-outline

Now, next to each trait, list five or six pieces of evidence from your life—things you've been or done—that prove your point.

Find patterns and connections

Group similar ideas and events together. For example, does your passion for numbers show up in your summer job at the computer store? Was basketball about sports or about friendships? Were there other times you did something challenging in order to be with people who matter to you?

Step 2: Drafting

Now it's time to get down to the actual writing. Write your essay in three basic parts:

- Introduction: Give your reader a brief idea of your essay's content. One vivid sentence might do: "The favorite science project was a complete failure."

- Body: Present the evidence that supports your main idea. Use narration and incident to show rather than tell.

- Conclusion: This can be just a few sentences to nail down the meaning of the events and incidents you've described.

But before you start writing, there are three basic essay styles you should consider:

Standard essay

Take two or three points from your self-outline, give a paragraph to each, and make sure you provide plenty of evidence. Choose things not apparent from the rest of your application or light up some of the activities and experiences listed there.

Less-is-more essay

In this format, you focus on a single interesting point about yourself. It works well for brief essays of a paragraph or half a page.

Narrative essay

A narrative essay tells a short and vivid story. Omit the introduction, write one or two narrative paragraphs that grab and engage the reader's attention, then explain what this little tale reveals about you.

Step 3: Editing

When you have a good draft, it's time to make final improvements, find and correct any errors, and get someone else to give you feedback. But remember, no one can speak for you; your own words and ideas are your best bet.

Let it cool

Take a break from your work and come back to it in a few days. Does your main idea come across clearly? Do you prove your points with specific details? Is your essay easy to read aloud?

Feedback time

Have someone you like and trust (but someone likely to tell you the truth) read your essay. Ask them to tell you what they think you're trying to convey. Did they get it right?

Edit down

Your language should be simple, direct, and clear. This is a personal essay, not a term paper. Make every word count (e.g., if you wrote "in society today," consider changing that to "now").

Proofread two more times

Careless spelling or grammatical errors, awkward language, or fuzzy logic will make your essay memorable—in a bad way.

Based on information found in *The College Application Essay,* **by Sarah Myers McGinty**

TIPS

Topic Brainstorming Worksheet

No matter what the essay question is, you're essentially being asked one thing: "Tell us about yourself." Brainstorming usually begins with a laundry list of ideas, good and bad, from which the best idea rises to the top. Here's a worksheet to help you brainstorm topics that will reveal something about yourself.

IN CHRONOLOGICAL ORDER, WHAT ARE THE FIVE MOST IMPORTANT EVENTS IN THE STORY OF YOUR LIFE?

1.
2.
3.
4.
5.

IF YOU WERE MAROONED ON A DESERT ISLAND, WHAT FIVE THINGS (BESIDES NECESSITIES) WOULD YOU WANT TO HAVE WITH YOU?

1.
2.
3.
4.
5.

WHAT FIVE ADJECTIVES OR PERSONALITY TRAITS WOULD YOUR FAMILY OR FRIENDS USE TO DESCRIBE YOU? (ASK IF YOU DON'T KNOW.)

1.
2.
3.
4.
5.

IF YOU HAD TO GIVE A SPEECH OR PRESENTATION, WHAT FIVE TOPICS WOULD YOU FEEL MOST CONFIDENT TALKING ABOUT?

1.
2.
3.
4.
5.

WHO ARE THE FIVE PEOPLE THAT YOU MOST ADMIRE?

1.
2.
3.
4.
5.

WHAT ARE YOUR FIVE MOST FAVORITE BOOKS OR MOVIES?

1.
2.
3.
4.
5.

WHAT ARE YOUR FIVE MOST FAVORITE MEMORIES?

1.
2.
3.
4.
5.

WHAT FIVE PEOPLE HAVE INFLUENCED YOU THE MOST?

1.
2.
3.
4.
5.

Essay Writing
Dos and Don'ts

A great essay will help you stand out from the other applicants, so take the time to do a good job on it. Check out these tips before you begin.

DO keep your focus narrow and personal

Your essay must prove a single point. Your main idea should be clear and easily followed from beginning to end. Ask someone to read just your introduction, and then tell you what your essay is about.

(And remember, it's about showing them who you are.)

DO back up what you say

Develop your main idea with specific facts, events, quotations, examples, and reasons.

Okay: "I like to be surrounded by people with a variety of backgrounds and interests."

Better: "During that night, I sang the theme song from *Casablanca* with a baseball coach who thinks he's Bogie, discussed Marxism with a little old lady, and heard more than I ever wanted to know about some woman's gall bladder operation."

DO give specifics

Avoid clichéd, generic, and predictable writing by using vivid and specific details.

Okay: "I have gotten so much out of life through the love and guidance of my family. I feel that many individuals have not been as fortunate; therefore, I would like to expand the lives of others."

Better: "My Mom and Dad stood on plenty of sidelines 'til their shoes filled with water or their fingers turned white, or somebody's golden retriever signed his name on their coats in mud. I think that kind of commitment is what I'd like to bring to working with fourth-graders."

DON'T tell them what you think they want to hear

Admission officers read plenty of essays about the charms of their university. Bring something new to the table.

DON'T write a résumé

Don't include information that is found elsewhere in the application. Your essay will end up sounding like an autobiography, travelogue, or laundry list. Yawn.

DON'T use 50 words when five will do

Eliminate unnecessary words.

Okay: "Over the years it has been pointed out to me by my parents, friends, and teachers—and I have even noticed it myself—that I am not the neatest person in the world."

Better: "I'm a slob."

DON'T forget to proofread

Typos and spelling or grammatical errors can be interpreted as carelessness or just bad writing. And don't rely on your computer's spell chick.[!]

Based on information found in *The College Application Essay*, by Sarah Myers McGinty

First Draft Checklist

Before you think you're satisfied with your first draft essay, use this checklist to do some essential "QC."

The good

- ☐ The essay reveals something insightful about yourself or your personality
- ☐ Introduction clearly states what the essay is about
- ☐ Used imagery to make your story vivid and memorable
- ☐ Varied your sentence structure (not all short, not all long, not all starting with "I")
- ☐ Used active verbs
- ☐ Single focus maintained throughout
- ☐ Has the right tone—honest and sincere
- ☐ Smooth transition between paragraphs
- ☐ Every point supported by examples
- ☐ Answered the essay question

The bad

- ☐ No plagiarized material (using another person's words without giving credit)
- ☐ No misspelled words (don't rely on spell-check)
- ☐ No run-on sentences or other grammatical errors
- ☐ Unnecessary words or sentences that do not support the main point
- ☐ Wrong facts—e.g., placed city in wrong country, attributed wrong book to author
- ☐ Referring to the wrong college if reusing essay from another application

The ugly

- ☐ Clichés or overused catchwords or phrases
- ☐ Boring "laundry list" of activities and accomplishments
- ☐ Reads like a generic essay—anyone could have written it
- ☐ Dumb jokes or gimmicky attempts to be clever
- ☐ Sarcasm or flippant tone
- ☐ Inappropriate language, slang, or anything in bad taste

10 Sample Essay Questions

As you start to think about how you should approach your college essay, it's good to have an idea of what types of essay questions colleges ask. Here are 10 recent examples:

1. **Duke University:** If you'd like to share a perspective you bring or experiences you've had to help us understand you better – perhaps related to a community you belong to, your sexual orientation or gender identity, or your family or cultural background – we encourage you to do so.

2. **Rice University:** While the choice of academic school you indicated is not binding, explain why you are applying to that particular school of study.

3. **Dartmouth College:** "It's not easy being green" was a frequent lament of Kermit the Frog. Discuss.

4. **LeHigh University:** You've just reached your one millionth hit on your YouTube video. What is the video about?

5. **Common Application:** Reflect on a time when you challenged a belief or idea. What prompted you to act? Would you make the same decision again?

6. **Common Application:** Recount an incident or time when you experienced failure. How did it affect you, and what did you learn from the experience?

7. **Boston College:** Share an example from a recent event when a leader or an average person faced a difficult choice. What were the consequences of the decision? Would you have done the same?

8. **University of Chicago:** Alice falls down the rabbit hole. Dorothy is swept up in the tornado. Neo takes the red pill. Don't tell us about another world you've imagined, tell us about its portal. Sure, the University of Chicago can be a portal, but please choose another.

9. **Pomona College:** Tell us about a subject that you couldn't stop exploring, a book you couldn't put down, or a Wikipedia rabbit hole you dove into. Why did it fascinate you?

10. **Brown University:** Why Brown?

NOTES

No-Sweat College Interviews

If You Have to Interview

A college interview is just a conversation where you learn about the college and the college learns about you. Just the same, it's normal to be a little nervous. These tips will help take the pressure off.

Know what type of interview it will be

Different schools use different types of interviews. You might sit down with an admission officer, a college student, a coach, or an alumnus. Or it might be less formal, such as group sessions with admission staff, or an online or phone interview.

Practice for it

Before you do the real thing, ask a family member or friend to help you practice. Take turns being the interviewer and the interviewee. That way, you'll get comfortable with both asking and answering questions. (There are lots of sample questions on pages 162 and 163.)

Relax—it's not a test

It's not the third degree. And there's no pass or fail. Unless you show up in a t-shirt and cut-offs and spew profanities, chances are the interview is not going to make or break you. As long as you've prepared and practiced, you'll make a good impression.

Remember that it can't hurt

Think of it this way: A bad interview won't hurt you, but a good interview can boost your chances. Look at it as an opportunity to put a personal face on your application, show your interest in the school, and learn more about whether the college is a good fit for you.

Come prepared with questions

Asking questions shows that you're interested in the college and in what the interviewer has to say. You don't want to be silent when asked, "What would you like to know about our college?" But don't ask obvious questions that you can answer on your own with a little research, like, "How many books are in the college library?" (See "20 Interview Questions You Might Be Asked" on page 162.)

Discuss any special circumstances

The interview is a good time to explain a hitch in your transcript or discuss any personal circumstances that affected your studies. Problems that you may find difficult to write about in the application are often easier to discuss with a sympathetic admission counselor.

Don't give it too much weight

Don't write off the college just because you think you had a bad interview. Interviewers have bad days, too. On the other hand, don't take it as a shoo-in if it goes really well.

If you can't relax

It's normal to feel nervous before an interview, especially if you've never done one before. These pointers will help you relax:

- Having everything ready and organized the night before is a great stress reliever. You'll sleep better knowing you won't have to rush around in the morning.

- Try to schedule your first interview at a "safety" school. That way you can break yourself in without feeling pressure.

- Bring a list of questions to ask. You don't have to memorize them. And it will help you keep perspective—you're buying, not selling.

- If you get butterflies in your stomach, take slow, regular breaths. Most people hold their breath when nervous, causing their stomach muscles to tighten up.

- If your palms get sweaty in the waiting room, sit with your palms facing up. That not only will keep them dry, but it also has a calming effect.

- Listen to your favorite music as you wait for the interview. Everyone has an "up" song— make sure it's in your playlist.

Some final dos and don'ts...

- Do dress neatly and comfortably. Business casual is a good choice.

- Don't bring a parent with you.

- Do turn off your phone.

- Do smile as you say hello.

- Don't tell the school it's your safety.

- Don't memorize speeches.

- Do write a thank-you note to the person who interviewed you.

TIPS

20 Interview Questions You Might Be Asked

A college interview is usually friendly and relaxed, but that doesn't mean you don't have to prepare. The following questions are good examples of what college interviewers typically ask.

1. What three adjectives would your best friend use to describe you?

2. What have you enjoyed most about your high school years?

3. How have you grown or changed?

4. What activities have you found most satisfying?

5. What things do you do well? What are your talents?

6. What strengths would you like most to develop?

7. Have any of your courses challenged you? Which ones? How?

8. What achievements are you most proud of?

9. How do you respond to academic pressure or competition?

10. What would you change about your school if you had the power?

11. What do you do for relaxation? For fun?

12. How do you define success?

13. How would you describe your family? Your community?

14. What do you want to accomplish in the years ahead?

15. What issues concern you?

16. Is there any book, article, or creative work that has had an impact on you?

17. Is there an author, activity, or field you've explored in depth?

18. How do you spend your summers?

19. If you had a year to do anything you wanted, what would you do?

20. Why are you interested in this college?

Based on information found in
Campus Visits & College Interviews,
by Zola Dincin Schneider

20 Questions for You to Ask Your Interviewer

A college interview is a two-way street—both you and the college are looking for information to help make an important decision. So when you are asked if you have any questions, be ready.

The following list of questions will help you think about what to ask:

1. What is unique or special about this college—the most compelling reason to enroll?

2. Which academic departments are the best?

3. What are the most popular majors on campus?

4. I am thinking of majoring in ___ . What can you tell me about how that's taught here?

5. Are there any special academic programs that you would recommend for me?

6. How would you describe the majority of students that go here?

7. What do students like most about this college?

8. What do they complain about the most?

9. Have there been any recent incidents I should know about?

10. What are the most popular extracurricular activities on campus?

11. Are commuter students involved in campus activities?

12. What are the weekends like?

13. What are the big campus events during the year?

14. What health services are offered on campus? What do students do when they get sick?

15. Are any major construction projects planned for the next four years?

16. How are roommates matched up?

17. Do many resident students live off campus?

18. Are there "themed" or other special housing options available? Is there one in particular that you think would be a good choice for me?

19. How does freshman registration work? How easy is it to get into the classes I want?

20. Are there any big changes coming that I should know about?

Interview Checklist

Use this checklist to make sure you are ready for the interview.

BEFORE

☐ Mark the date and time of the interview appointment on your calendar.

☐ Find out what type of interview it will be—such as a student interview versus an alumni interview.

☐ Learn what you can about the college. (Check collegeboard.org and the college's website.)

☐ Make notes about why you are interested in this college.

☐ Review the questions an interviewer might ask and think about what your answers will be.

☐ Prepare questions to ask the interviewer.

☐ Do a practice interview.

☐ Get directions to the college's campus and admission office.

☐ Choose an appropriate interview outfit.

☐ Gather any documents you might need, such as your test scores and high school transcript.

DURING

☐ Be on time. But if you are delayed, call ahead and give an estimated time of arrival.

☐ Be yourself, and be honest.

☐ Stay calm and be polite.

☐ Answer the questions, but don't ramble or give more info than asked for.

☐ Ask questions of your own that will help you decide if the college is right for you.

☐ End with a smile and a firm handshake.

AFTER

☐ Make notes about the conversation to preserve what you learned, thank-you note material, or follow-up questions.

☐ Send a thank-you letter or e-mail to the interviewer and refer to something you discussed.

The
Money Part

Senior Year Financial Aid Timeline

Applying for financial aid is a process of its own, and the deadlines often don't track your college admission deadlines. Use this timeline to stay on top of it all, but be sure to check the specific requirements and deadlines of the colleges you are applying to.

SUMMER BEFORE SENIOR YEAR

Research scholarship opportunities that you might be eligible for. By starting now you can be sure to find programs before their deadlines have passed, and you'll have enough time to prepare a complete, competitive application.

SEPTEMBER

- **Get an FSA ID** for both yourself and one of your parents from **www.fafsa.ed.gov**. You'll need them to submit the FAFSA financial aid form, which you can submit any time after October 1.

- **Ask your school counselor about local scholarships** offered by church groups, civic associations, and businesses in your area.

- Find out if there will be a **family financial aid night** at your high school or elsewhere in your area.

- If you are going to apply **Early Decision** to a college, ask that college if they have forms for an early estimate of your financial aid eligibility.

OCTOBER

- **Start working on your FAFSA** and submit it as soon as you can. Go to **www.fafsa.ed.gov** to access the form.

- If you need to fill out the **CSS Profile**, you can do so on the PROFILE ONLINE Web site starting Oct. 1.

- **If any scholarship applications require recommendations**, you should request them now, or at least four weeks in advance of the deadline.

NOVEMBER

- Use the **online financial aid calculator** on collegeboard.org to estimate your family's expected family contribution (EFC).

- If need be, correct or update your **Student Aid Report (SAR)** that follows the FAFSA.

DECEMBER

- **Contact the financial aid office** at the colleges on your list to make sure you have all required **financial aid forms**.

- **Apply for scholarships** in time to meet application deadlines.

JANUARY

- If a college you're applying to has an **early financial aid priority date**, submit your FAFSA as soon as you can if you haven't already. Some colleges priority dates can be as early as Feb. 1.

- **Submit other financial aid forms** that may be required—such as the CSS Profile or the college's own forms. Keep copies.

FEBRUARY

- **Double check** that you are on track to meet all financial aid requirements, priority dates, and deadlines for the colleges on your "short list." (See the "Financial Aid Application Tracker" on p. 170).

- If you submitted the **CSS Profile, check your acknowledgment** and send any corrections, if necessary, directly to the colleges that require it.

- You and/or your parents should file your **income tax returns early** this year. Some colleges might want to see more current tax information before finalizing financial aid offers.

MARCH

- If necessary, write to the financial aid offices of your colleges to alert them to any **special circumstances** that affect your family's ability to pay for college, such as a job loss or high health care costs.

- Submit any **additional documentation** (such as State tax returns) that may be required.

- Send copies of your **FAFSA to any scholarship programs** that require it as part of their applications.

APRIL

- Most admission decisions and financial aid award letters arrive this month. **Carefully compare financial aid award letters** from the colleges that accept you.

- Text, e-mail, or call the colleges if you have any **questions about the financial aid packages** they've offered you. Make sure you understand all terms and conditions.

- If you didn't get enough aid to be able to attend a particular college, consider your options, which includes appealing the award.

- Make a final decision, **accept the aid package and mail a deposit check** to the college you select before May 1 (the acceptance deadline for most schools).

- On the waiting list at your first-choice college? Don't let that cause you to lose your aid at another college that has accepted you. **Accept that award** in case you don't make it off the waiting list.

MAY

- Consider applying for non-need-based **loans** to cover your family's out-of-pocket college expenses. See "Your College Loan Options" on page 184, and "10 Essential Borrowing Tips" on page 186.

- **Thank everyone** who wrote you recommendations or otherwise helped with your scholarship applications.

JUNE

Think about your summer job options. The more money you make, the easier it will be to finance college—and have some fun during the school year.

Financial Aid Application Tracker

This tracker will help you stay on top of all the forms and deadlines involved in applying for financial aid. Put in all due dates, and check off when done. Use it together with the "College Application Tracker" on page 126. Be sure to save copies of everything before submitting.

		COLLEGE 1	COLLEGE 2
School codes	Federal code		
	CSS Profile code		
Deadlines	Priority date		
	Closing date		
FAFSA	Required? (date submitted)		
	Listed college codes on FAFSA and/or SAR		
	Used IRS Data Retrieval tool to upload tax info		
CSS Profile	Required? (date submitted)		
	School code submitted to College Board		
	Submitted supplemental forms (if necessary)		
	Paid fee to have report sent to college		
	Sent corrections to college(s) (if necessary)		
Other forms required?	State aid form (date submitted)		
	College's own form (date submitted)		
	Application for scholarship (date submitted)		
	Any other forms required		
After applying	Need to send letter explaining special circumstance?		
	Additional documentation required?		
	Spoke to financial aid office?		
	Received award letter		
	Reply date deadline		
	Accepted award		

COLLEGE 3	COLLEGE 4	COLLEGE 5	COLLEGE 6	COLLEGE 7	COLLEGE 8
SCHOOL NAME	SCHOOL NAME	SCHOOL NAME	SCHOOL NAME	SCHOOL NAME	SCHOOL NAME

10 Questions for the Financial Aid Office

Each college has its own set of rules and policies governing financial aid—how outside scholarships are treated, whether aid awards can be appealed—information that may or may not appear in their brochures. As you check out the colleges on your list, you'll need to find out the details.

Here are 10 questions to get you started:

1. What's the projected total cost of attendance (tuition and fees, books and supplies, room and board, travel, and other personal expenses) for the next four years?

2. By how much should I expect my costs to increase each year? How much have tuition, fees, room and board increased over the last three to five years?

3. Does financial need have an impact on admission decisions? How is financial aid affected if I apply via an Early Decision or Early Action program?

4. Are there any scholarships available that aren't based on financial need? Do I need to complete a separate application for merit-based scholarships?

5. What is the priority deadline to apply for financial aid?

6. When will I be notified about financial aid award decisions?

7. If the financial aid package isn't enough, can I appeal? Under what conditions, if any, will the aid office reconsider the offer?

8. How will the aid package change from year to year? What will happen if my family's financial situation changes? What will happen if my enrollment status (or that of a family member) changes?

9. What are the academic requirements or other conditions for the renewal of financial aid, including scholarships?

10. When can I expect to receive bills from the college? Is there an option to spread the yearly payment over equal monthly installments?

Fill Out the FAFSA Step-by-Step

Just about every college financial aid program requires the FAFSA, or Free Application for Federal Student Aid, even if they also require other forms. Most schools and states use nothing but the FAFSA to determine eligibility for aid.

You have probably heard that the FAFSA is complicated, but it's actually pretty easy to fill out. Go to www.fafsa.ed.gov to get started.

The following outline will help you walk through it. (While the wording and order of the questions may change from year to year, the substance remains more or less the same.) Skip logic will show you only those questions that apply to you, so you might not see all the questions described here.

First, a few general points to keep in mind about the FAFSA:

- You can submit your FAFSA anytime after Oct. 1 of the year before you'll start college. Just keep in mind that many college deadlines for financial aid are in March, and some are in February.

- Don't be fooled by the FAFSA deadline of June 30; it's the college deadlines that count.

- If you don't have Internet access or just prefer to work on paper, you can request the paper FAFSA by calling 1-877-433-7827. After you submit the paper FAFSA, you'll have to allow at least four weeks for mailing and processing before your earliest deadline.

- Before you submit online, you need to get an FSA ID for both yourself and for one of your parents from www.fafsa.ed.gov so that the form can be signed electronically.

- After you submit your FAFSA, you will receive a Student Aid Report (SAR), summarizing the information you supplied on the FAFSA. You can then correct errors online.

> Go to **www.fafsa.ed.gov** to file the FAFSA online.

Step One: Questions About Yourself

These questions gather basic information used to identify you and determine which federal and state programs you may qualify for. For example, the question about your citizenship is there because only U.S. citizens (or eligible noncitizens) can get federal student aid. While many of these questions seem obvious, here are some helpful points:

Your name: Enter this *exactly* as it appears on your social security card. If the two don't match, it will slow down the whole process.

Your social security number: Required. You won't be able to access the online form without one, and if you submit the paper form without one, it will be returned to you unprocessed. If you make an error entering this number on the login page, you can't change it and you have to start a new FAFSA. More delay.

Your date of birth: That's easy enough.

Male students 18 years or older: You must be registered with the Selective Service (the draft) in order to be eligible for federal aid. If you're not registered, do it now on the FAFSA.

Your state of legal residence: This might be different from where you are living at the time you fill out the form. If you have residences in more than one state or move around a lot, ask your colleges how that affects you.

File your FAFSA as early as you can. When it comes to financial aid, time really is money. Those who apply late get less, or none.

Your e-mail address: This is optional, but you should provide it. Use an e-mail address you check regularly. You won't get spam and will receive your SAR by e-mail instead of snail mail, saving lots of time.

Your citizenship: An "eligible noncitizen" is someone holding a green card (Permanent Resident Card), or someone who has refugee status. It is not someone visiting on a student visa. If you're neither a citizen nor an eligible noncitizen, you can't get federal aid, but you might be eligible for other types of aid. Ask the colleges you are applying to if you should still fill out the FAFSA.

Whether you've ever been convicted of possessing or selling illegal drugs: Say "yes" only if the offense occurred while you were receiving federal student aid (unlikely if this is your first FAFSA), it's still on your record, and you were tried as an adult.

Your high school completion status next year: Select "high school diploma" if you will graduate from a public or private high school this year; "General Educational Development (GED)" if you have a GED diploma or expect to pass the exam; and "home-schooled" if you will satisfy your state's requirements for completing home schooling at the high school level. If the answer for you is "none of the above," contact the financial aid office at the colleges you want to attend.

Name and address of your high school: You will be asked for this if you selected "high school diploma" in the previous question. The online FAFSA provides a search tool to find your high school and auto-fill, but if you can't find it there you can just enter in the info.

What grade level will you be in next school year: "Grade" means year of college.

What degree will you be working on in the next school year: If you're not sure (for example, if you're applying to both two-year and four-year colleges), check "undecided."

The highest level of education completed by your parents: This won't affect your federal aid, but some states use this information to award scholarships to students who are the first in their family to attend college.

Whether you're interested in work-study: The best answer is "yes." Preserve your options. You're not committing to anything, and your answer won't affect the amount of grant money you might get.

Step Two: College Selection

This is where you say which colleges should receive your FAFSA information. You list the colleges, and the government will send the processed information to them for free.

Identify the colleges by federal school code. The online FAFSA provides a search tool for you to find the code. If you are filing a paper FAFSA, you can find the code on collegeboard.org's College Search, at www.fafsa.ed.gov, or the colleges' financial aid websites.

You can list up to 10 colleges online; but if you are using the paper FAFSA, you can only list four. In either case, you can add additional schools later, but when choosing which colleges to list first, *pick the ones whose financial aid deadlines come first.*

If you use the apaper FAFSA, you can only list four colleges to receive your information. You can add up to six more later, but you'll have to wait until your FAFSA is processed.

For each college, you have to say whether you plan to live on campus, off campus, or with your parents. Your answer will affect the housing costs that the school will estimate for you, and therefore your financial need. If you haven't made a decision yet, assume you'll live on campus.

Step Three: Your Dependency Status

These questions are meant to determine if you are independent of your parents for purposes of federal financial aid. Interestingly, it doesn't matter if you are supporting yourself or whether your parents claim you as a dependent on their tax return. If you can truthfully answer "yes" to even one of the questions in this step, you will be considered independent.

If you are independent, then you can skip the next step, which asks about your parents' income and assets. *But there are certain cases where a college will want to know about your parents' finances anyway.* It's a good idea to ask the colleges to which you're applying whether they'll consider you fully independent for the purpose of awarding you money from their own funds. If one or more of them won't, you should provide your parents' information.

Step Four: Questions About Your Parents

Modern family life can make the definition of "parent" complicated. But the FAFSA definitions are fairly clear (stepparents count; legal guardians and foster parents don't, unless they have legally adopted you).

Marital status: Indicate the status as it is at the time you submit the form.

Their social security numbers: Unlike you, your parents are not required to have social security numbers in order for you to file the FAFSA. (But in that case you have to enter zeroes.) If they do have social security numbers, they must provide them.

Their names: Again, if they have social security cards, their names must exactly match.

The number of people in your parents' household: These include you and your parents. The number in your household who will be in college during the next year is also asked for; this includes you (but *not* your parents). These questions affect how much money your parents will be expected to contribute to your education.

Step Five: Questions About Your Parents' Finances

This step is easy if your parents filed a tax return for the year in question (2016 if you will start college in the fall of 2018). Here's a rundown of the important questions:

If either parent is a "dislocated worker": Answer "yes" if one (or both) of your parents is unemployed because of a layoff or loss of a business. You should also let the financial aid office know at each college to which you are applying.

Whether anyone in the household received certain federal benefits. A "yes" answer to any of the listed programs, such as free or reduced-price lunch or SNAP assistance (food stamps), will likely result in a determination that your family should not be expected to contribute any money toward your education.

Whether they're eligible to file the 1040A or 1040EZ tax form: The instructions that come with the FAFSA explain who can file these forms. If they can, it's to your advantage to say "yes," no matter what tax form they actually use.

> Most colleges prefer that the **IRS Data Retrieval Process** be used to provide tax data on the FAFSA. If that's not possible (perhaps they didn't file a return), check with your colleges to see how to best provide this information.

Their income tax information: The FAFSA asks for the tax information for the year that is two-years prior to your first year of college (e.g., 2016 if you will start college in fall 2018). The **IRS Data Retrieval Process** makes it simple; accessible right from the online FAFSA, this tool will import the information directly from the filed return.

Besides income from working and interest payments, they will also have to report:

- Untaxed income such as welfare benefits, Social Security benefits, or child support.

- Contributions your parents or their employers made last year to tax-deferred retirement plans such as Individual Retirement Accounts (IRAs), 401(k)s, or Keogh accounts.

What their assets are: These include cash, savings, and the value of investments, such as stocks and bonds. The amounts to put down are "as of" the day you fill out the FAFSA. Often that is just a best guess, using the most recent bank statements. (Keep in mind that the amount of aid to which you are entitled is based much more on family income than on assets.)

A few points about investments:

- They do not include the home where your parents primarily live (a summer cottage would be included), a family-owned business of less than 100 employees, or a family farm that they live on and operate.

- They also do not include the value of life insurance or retirement accounts, such as IRAs, 401(k)s, Keogh plans, and the like.

- Your parents do have to include, however, the current balance of any prepaid tuition or college savings accounts (such as 529 plans) they (not you) own.

Step Six: Your Own Income and Assets

These questions ask about *your* income and assets—whether or not you are independent. Income is how much money you made from working; assets are what you own and the savings you have. If you are married, they also want to know about your spouse's income and assets.

This section is mostly a repeat of Step Five, with the difference that the questions are about your finances instead of your parents'. Some additional points:

- Be sure to say "yes," if you can, to the question about your eligibility to file the 1040A or 1040EZ tax form.

- The questions about the number of people in your household mean *your* household, if you have one—not your parents' household.

- Don't include any college savings accounts in this step unless you are independent (you answered "yes" to any question in Step Two), and they are owned by you in your own name.

Step Seven: Review Your Answers, Then Sign and Submit

This is easy, but there are still some points to know:

- This is a really important form, so take the time to carefully review all your answers for accuracy and spelling—even your name.

- Use your FSA IDs to sign electronically—don't use the "print signature page and mail" option. It just wastes time.

- If your parents provided financial information, one of them also needs to sign.

- You'll see a list of terms you must agree to by signing. Nothing is onerous here, but there is a scary penalty for giving false or misleading information. This does not mean honest mistakes or estimates that turn out to be way off— they're talking about intentional fraud.

- Be sure to keep clicking on "next" until you get to the confirmation page—only then is your FAFSA actually submitted.

> Avoid any website that offers to help you file the FAFSA for a fee. The federal government offers its help for free and does not endorse any site that charges money for assistance.

Step Eight: Confirmation

You're done! Be sure to print the confirmation page and the application information, and save it to your hard drive as well. If you don't have a printer, write down the confirmation number, date and time, and keep it safe—it's your proof that your FAFSA was received.

If you file using the paper form, make a photocopy of it before mailing it, and keep that photocopy together with the worksheets you filled out and all the records you used.

Making corrections after you file

If the processed information on your Student Aid Report (SAR) is not accurate, then you must make corrections. It's easy to do—just go back to www.fafsa.ed.gov, log in, and click on "Make FAFSA Corrections." You can also add or remove colleges this way.

Remember, you can only correct information that was wrong as of the date that you signed and submitted your FAFSA (usually because you provided estimates). Don't make changes because of changed circumstances, such as a job loss. If something like that happens, let the colleges know about it directly. Send a letter of explanation to the financial aid office, and follow up with a phone call.

Fill Out the CSS Profile™ Step-by-Step

Some colleges require an additional form besides the FAFSA: The CSS/Financial Aid PROFILE®. The CSS Profile is administered by the College Board, a not-for-profit association of schools and colleges (and the publisher of this book).

Schools that require the CSS Profile do so because it gives a more complete account of your financial situation, which helps them award aid from their own funds. For that reason, the CSS Profile is a bit longer than the FAFSA, and some colleges might even ask for more information after the form is filed.

Create Your Account and File Early

If you are applying to a college that requires the CSS Profile, it's best to get it done well before your colleges' deadlines. It's best to submit the CSS Profile at least one week before your earliest financial aid priority date.

Because the CSS Profile use the same tax year information as the FAFSA for a majority of its questions, it may be helpful to fill it out soon after you complete the FAFSA. But if you have to submit the CSS Profile before you have the most recent tax return information, use estimates, and then send corrections to the college later if necessary.

> The CSS Profile is available online only. If you can't access it at home, use a computer at your school or local library.

Documents You'll Need Before You Fill It Out

You'll need these records for both yourself and your parents:

- Federal income tax return for the year before you start college (2017 if you will start college in fall 2018), if completed, or pay stubs and other income-related records for estimates
- Federal income tax return for the year before that (2016 if you will start college in fall 2018)
- W-2 forms and other records of money earned for those two years
- Records of untaxed income for those two years
- Current bank statements and mortgage information
- Records of stocks, bonds, trusts, and other investments

So let's get started. As you fill out the form, don't be surprised if you don't see all the steps that are discussed here. Like most online forms, the CSS Profile won't show you questions that don't apply to you.

Step 1: Your Basic Information

The form begins by asking for some basic information about you, such as your date of birth, where you live, whether you are a U.S. citizen, a veteran, married, etc. Some of these questions are intended to clarify whether you're a dependent or an independent student.

Step 2: College Information

This section lets you select which colleges should receive your CSS Profile application. You can add more colleges or programs later if need be.

Step 3: Parents' Information

This section asks your parents to provide information about themselves, including name, date of birth, employment status, and whether they themselves are in college or graduate school. Some of these questions have to do with clarifying financial strength—for example, the question about what kind of retirement plans your parents have.

Step 4: Parents' Income and Benefits for the "Prior-Prior" Year

Here your parents are asked to report their income and benefits from two years before the year you intend to start college. That should be the same tax information you used to complete your FAFSA. If your parents have the tax return for that year on hand, they just have to copy from the right lines.

Step 5: Parents' Income and Benefits for the Prior Year

In this section, your parents give information about their income and benefits for the year before you intend to start college (e.g., 2017 if you will begin college fall 2018). If you're up against a deadline and your parents haven't yet done that tax return, they should just estimate the amounts.

Step 6: Parents' Anticipated Income and Benefits

Your parents are asked here to estimate how much they expect to receive in income and benefits during the year in which you start college, and to explain any unusual increases or decreases in income and benefits (10 percent or more) from the prior year.

Step 7: Parent Income Not Reported on Taxes

Some forms of income don't show up on tax forms. This section asks if there are other sources of income that your family is receiving.

Step 8: Parent Address Information

In this section your parents are asked for some additional information about your family's residence(s) and housing.

Step 9: Parents' Assets

This section asks about cash, savings, and checking accounts. If they own their home, there are questions about home equity (the difference between current market value and any outstanding mortgage debt). There are also questions about other assets they might own, such as investments, businesses, farms, other real estate, any retirement accounts, and any educational savings accounts that they've opened for you or your siblings.

Step 10: Parents' Expenses

The types of expenses included here are child support payments, certain educational costs, and medical and dental expenses not covered by insurance. Don't include ordinary expenses like grocery bills.

Step 11: Information About a Noncustodial Parent

If your parents are divorced or separated, this section asks for information about the parent who doesn't have custody of you. But it should be filled out by your custodial parent. If such information is unavailable, there is a place to explain why. Colleges may request that the noncustodial parent fill out a supplemental form.

Step 12: Your Own Income and Benefits for Last Year

This section asks about your income and benefits in the year before you intend to start college. If you have a completed tax return for that year, this section is mostly a matter of copying the info. If you had income or benefits but didn't file a return, there's a worksheet available for you to tally it up.

Step 13: Your Expected Summer/School-Year Resources for the Coming School Year

Here you're asked to state your expected resources for the upcoming summer and school year. You're also asked about scholarships you expect to get from sources other than the colleges to which you're applying.

This may seem like a strange series of questions, especially if you don't know yet where you'll be going to college next year, or where (even if) you'll be working. Do the best you can to estimate these figures. If you're not sure how to answer, check the CSS Profile help online or contact the financial aid office at the college to which you're applying.

Step 14: Your Own Assets

You need to list any cash you have and any checking or savings accounts in your name. You should also include any investments, such as certificates of deposit, savings bonds, stocks, or real estate that you own.

If you have any trust accounts, list their value here and answer the questions about them. But don't include money in Section 529 prepaid tuition plans; those aren't the same as trusts.

Step 15: Your Expenses for the Prior Year

You will only see these questions if you're an independent student. If so, you'll be asked about any child support you or your spouse paid to a former spouse and any medical and dental expenses you had last year that weren't covered by insurance.

Step 16: Household Summary

This section asks questions about dependent members of your household other than your parents. The information is used to determine how much family income should be allocated for educating all its members.

Step 17: Explanations/Special Circumstances

This section gives you a chance to explain anything unusual in your application or any special circumstances that affect your family's ability to pay for college, such as unusually high medical or dental expenses, or loss of employment. You should also give information about any outside scholarships you've been awarded.

If you have a question about the CSS Profile and can't find an answer in the online help, there is an additional help line: e-mail **help@cssprofile.org** or call **305-829-9793**.

You should also use this section to complete answers from previous sections if there wasn't an explanation box provided (for example, to provide details about a gift from a relative).

You're limited to 2,000 characters (about 300 words) in this section. If you need more space, send the information on paper directly to your colleges, including your name and social security number on all correspondence.

Step 18: Supplemental Information

You will only see this section if one or more of the colleges to which you're applying requires more information.

After Submitting Your CSS Profile

You'll receive an online acknowledgment that confirms the colleges to which you're sending the information and gives you the opportunity to review any data you submitted. Once you submit your CSS Profile, you can't revise your information online. You should print the acknowledgment and use it to make changes, and send any corrections directly to your colleges.

Compare Your Awards Worksheet

Your final college choice may depend upon which one offers the most financial aid. Award letters often look different, so use this worksheet to compare them "apples to apples."

	COLLEGE 1	COLLEGE 2	COLLEGE 3	COLLEGE 4
GRANTS AND SCHOLARSHIPS				
• Federal				
• State				
• College				
• Other (include outside scholarships you got on your own)				
Percentage of package that is grant/scholarship	%	%	%	%
LOANS/WORK-STUDY				
• Subsidized Stafford loan (Government pays the interest while you are in school.)				
• Unsubsidized Stafford loan (You pay all the interest.)				
• Perkins loan (low-interest federal loan)				
• Other (Remember, parent PLUS loans are available to everyone and should not be considered financial aid.)				
• Work-study (How much will you earn for the year?)				
Percentage of package that is loans/work	%	%	%	%
a) Total cost (tuition, fees, room and board, books and supplies, travel, personal expenses)				
b) Total financial aid award				
c) Net cost to attend (a minus b)				

Questions to Ask About Your Financial Aid Award

Here are some questions you should ask your college financial aid office before you accept your award:

If you're awarded a grant or scholarship:

1. What do I have to do to keep my scholarship?

2. Is there a minimum GPA or other condition?

3. Do I have to do anything more than maintain satisfactory grades?

4. Is the scholarship renewable in subsequent years?

5. If I win an outside scholarship, what happens to my aid?

If you're awarded a loan:

1. What are the terms of my loan?

2. What is the interest rate, and when do I start repayment?

3. How much will I owe by the time I graduate?

4. What will my monthly repayment be?

5. By how much will my loan increase after my first year?

If you're awarded work-study:

1. Do I have a "guaranteed" job, or will I have to find one?

2. How are jobs assigned?

3. How many hours per week will I be expected to work?

4. What is the hourly wage?

5. Will I be paid directly, or will my student account get credited?

Your College Loan Options

Did you know that almost 40 percent of all financial aid comes in the form of loans? Some loans are need-based—meaning they're only given to families who can't pay the full cost of the college. Other loans don't require a showing of financial need.

Need-based loans tend to have better terms, so you should consider those loans first.

Federal student loans

There are three main types of federal student loans:

Subsidized Stafford loans are need-based loans with interest rates in the 4–6 percent range. They are interest free until you graduate; that's because the federal government pays the interest for you while you're in school. This is why they're called subsidized loans.

Unsubsidized Stafford loans aren't based on financial need and can be used to help pay the family share of costs. With an unsubsidized Stafford loan, you'll be charged only the interest portion of the loan while you're in school. You can choose to make those interest payments while you are in school, or you can let the interest accrue (accumulate) and not make any payments until after you graduate. But if you do that, the amount of the accrued interest is added to the loan, meaning that you will repay more money overall.

> When you start paying back your educational loan, remember that the interest may be tax deductible.

Perkins loans are another type of subsidized need-based loan and are awarded at the discretion of the college financial aid office to students with the highest need. The interest rate is very low and you don't make any loan payments while in school. Perkins-loan debt may be forgiven if you enter a career in the public service, such as teaching.

Other student loan options

Private student loans: A number of lenders offer private education loans to students. These loans are not subsidized and usually carry a higher interest rate than federal loans. But, they usually have lower interest rates than other consumer loans, and may have attractive features, such as deferred repayment while in school. Your parents or some other creditworthy person might have to co-sign the loan.

College-sponsored loans: Some colleges lend money to students directly from their own funds. Interest rates may be lower than federal student loans. Read the college's financial aid information to find out if these are available.

State loans: Some states sponsor loan programs for students (and parents) who are state residents. These loans are usually neither subsidized nor based on need. Check with your state financial aid agency to find out more.

Other loans: Besides setting up scholarships, some private organizations and foundations have loan programs as well. Borrowing terms may be quite favorable. You can use collegeboard.org's Scholarship Search program to find these.

Parent loans

Parents also have federal, private, and college-sponsored loan options.

Federal PLUS loans: This program is the largest source of parent loans. Your parents can borrow up to the full cost of attendance minus any financial aid you receive, and repayment starts 60 days after money is paid to the college. To get a PLUS loan, your parents have to fill out an application and pass a credit review.

Private parent loans: A number of lenders and other financial institutions offer private education loans for parents. These loans usually carry a higher interest rate than PLUS Loans.

College-sponsored loans: A small number of colleges offer their own parent loans, usually at a better rate than PLUS. Check each college's financial aid materials to see if such loans are available.

Home-equity loans: Your parents might consider taking out a loan against their home equity. While this may be an attractive option, you should keep in mind that home-equity loans come with the condition that if they can't pay back the loan, the bank can foreclose on their house.

What if you can't make the payments?

If you take out a federal loan, you'll have several repayment plans to choose from. The standard plan has fixed monthly payments over a ten-year term. But other plans offer "pay as you earn" options that keep the monthly payments within a percentage (e.g. 10%) of your after-tax income, and recalculate the payments each year based on your updated income and/or family size. The term of the loan might be longer, but it's still a pretty good deal.

If you run into economic hardship, you can postpone your loan payments by applying for a deferment (during which no interest accumulates) or forbearance (during which it does). In some circumstances, such as total disability or teaching in a designated low-income school, the loan can be cancelled. These rules apply to all federal student loans, but not to PLUS loans.

For private loans, you might be able to work out a new schedule of payments that you can handle; but that will probably increase the total amount you will have to repay.

10 Essential Borrowing Tips

Just about everybody has to borrow money for college. But taking on loans can be intimidating because you're betting you'll make enough money after graduation to pay them back, and you may not feel sure of that. But a college degree will definitely increase your earning power, so it should be a safe bet.

Still, don't take it lightly. Follow these tips and you won't get in over your head.

1. **Don't do anything until you've looked at your financial aid award.** Figure out which need-based loans you have been given and for what amounts. These loans will have better terms than what you can get on your own.

2. **Do the math.** After you look at your full financial picture—total college cost, the amount of financial aid you received, and what your family can contribute—settle on an amount you actually need to borrow.

3. **Get advice.** If you feel you need to borrow more than the amount that's been offered in your award letter, talk with a financial aid counselor before taking on an additional loan.

4. **Never borrow more than you need.** Remember, you're not required to borrow the full amount of a loan you've been offered in your financial aid award, or to borrow the maximum loan amount.

5. **Don't forget about student employment as an alternative for borrowing.** Although working at a job can seem like an extra burden, so is struggling with high loan repayments after college.

6. **Apply for your loan right away.** You want to make sure that the loan is approved and the money paid to the college before you have to make your first student account payment.

7. **Follow the loan application instructions carefully.** Any mistakes you make will delay receipt of the funds.

8. **Don't forget the fees.** For Direct Stafford loans, a one percent loan fee will be subtracted from the loan before the check is sent to your college. Direct Plus loans have higher fees, usually around 4 percent.

9. **Keep track of your "loan tab"**— what your monthly repayment amount will be after graduation. There is a "Student Loan Calculator" on collegeboard.org that will do the math for you.

10. **For unsubsidized loans, consider making interest payments while in school.** They won't be much and will save you money—you'll end up having to pay back significantly less than if you delay (and capitalize) the interest payments.

Finding Scholarships

With thousands of scholarships out there, finding ones that you have a chance of winning can seem like looking for a needle in a haystack. Here are some tips to help you zero in on the scholarships worth going for.

Start looking as soon as you can

It's best to start in the spring of your junior year—you'll be surprised how fast deadlines will creep up on you. You'll also need time to prepare a complete, competitive application.

Match yourself to eligibility requirements

The first step is to create a list of things about yourself that scholarship programs might be looking for. (The "Scholarship Matchmaker" on page 188 will help you with that.) Then use your list to form queries in search programs like Scholarship Search on collegeboard.org.

Think locally

It's a sure bet that many businesses and organizations in your community are sponsoring scholarships for hometown students. Most will offer just a few hundred dollars—enough to buy a semester's worth of textbooks. But your chances of receiving an award are much higher than they are for the big national competitions.

Ask your school counselor about local scholarship programs. (There may even be a scholarship for graduates of your high school.) You should also check with your church, temple, or mosque; the local chamber of commerce; and any civic clubs that your family are members of.

Look to your state

Almost every state has a scholarship program for residents—usually limited to students who attend college in-state.

Don't cast too wide a net

Remember that applying for scholarships will be a lot of work! It's better to invest your time applying to a few scholarships that closely match your characteristics and interests than it is to pursue a lot of longshots. If you're having trouble narrowing down your search, consider the following:

- **How many applicants are there each year?** Knowing the ratio between the number of applicants and the number of awards given out will help you gauge your chances.

- **Is this really for me?** Don't force yourself to fulfill application requirements that will be a pain. Focus, instead, on scholarships that appeal to you or sound like fun.

- **Can I live with the strings attached?** Some scholarships or loan forgiveness programs have service requirements (like teaching for a year in a rural or inner-city district after college). And some summer internships will require you to move to another city.

Scholarship Matchmaker

Use this worksheet to match yourself to scholarship eligibility requirements.
It's a great way to get ready to use search programs like Scholarship Search on
collegeboard.org.

YOUR BASICS

GENDER   STATE OF RESIDENCE

MINORITY STATUS (e.g., African American, Alaskan Native)

NATIONALITY OR ETHNIC BACKGROUND (e.g., Chinese, Greek)

RELIGIOUS AFFILIATION

SPECIAL QUALS

LEARNING OR PHYSICAL DISABILITY

MILITARY SERVICE is the basis of many scholarships, and not just for those who served, but also for their spouses and children, or even just
descendants of a veteran. Some are related to specific conflicts. Talk to your family about its military history. (Was Grandpa in the Korean War?)

NAME OF VETERAN	BRANCH	CONFLICT
NAME OF VETERAN	BRANCH	CONFLICT
NAME OF VETERAN	BRANCH	CONFLICT

ACADEMIC GOALS (Even if you are "undecided" at this point, you should list all the majors/careers you are leaning toward.)

MAJOR   CAREER

☐ STUDY ABROAD? (There are scholarships to help you pay for it—check here to remind yourself to seek them out.)

WHO YOU KNOW

ORGANIZATIONS AND ASSOCIATIONS (e.g., Kiwanis, Rotary, Elks Club)

EMPLOYERS AND CORPORATIONS (List the companies that you or someone in your family works for.)

How to Spot a Scholarship Scam

If researching scholarships sounds like too much work, you may think it's a good idea to use a paid scholarship search service. If you do, please be careful. Some of these services do a responsible job for a modest fee, but many make unrealistic claims and charge a lot of money. Some are outright fraudulent, and some are even fronts for criminal identity theft operations.

The Federal Trade Commission (FTC) developed "Project $cholar$cam" to alert students and families about potential scams and how to recognize them. Here are the FTC's six basic warning signs:

"The scholarship is guaranteed or your money back." No one can guarantee that they'll get you a grant or a scholarship. And refund guarantees often have strings attached.

"You can't get this information anywhere else." Legitimate scholarship programs are eager to give money to qualified students. They are not interested in keeping the money a secret.

"I just need your credit card or bank account number to hold this scholarship." Never, ever give your credit card number, social security number, or bank account information to someone who called you unsolicited. It may be the setup for identity theft.

> For more information go to **www.FinAid.org** for advice on how to identify scams, how to distinguish between legitimate and fraudulent organizations, and what to do if you are scammed.

"We'll do all the work." Don't be fooled. There's no way around it. You must apply for scholarships or grants yourself.

"The scholarship will cost money." Don't pay anyone who claims to be "holding" a scholarship or grant for you. Free money shouldn't cost a thing.

"You've been selected by a national foundation" to receive a scholarship or "You're a finalist" in a contest you never entered.

Before you send money to apply for a scholarship, check it out. Make sure the foundation or program is legitimate.

If you suspect a scam, bring a copy of all literature and correspondence to your guidance office. You can also contact the Better Business Bureau, your State Bureau of Consumer Protection, your State Attorney General's Office, or report the offer to the National Fraud Information Center.

Scholarship Application Tracker

This tracker will help you stay on top of all the requirements, paperwork, and deadlines you'll need to meet when applying for scholarships. Put in all due dates, and check off when done.

		SCHOLARSHIP 1	SCHOLARSHIP 2
Type of award (scholarship, internship, loan)			
Amount of award			
Application deadline			
Eligibility requirements	Academics (GPA, class rank, etc.)		
	Employment/membership		
	Ethnic/minority/religious		
	Major or career interest		
	Military		
	Residency		
	Other		
Forms required	Application		
	FAFSA		
	High school transcript		
	Proof/documentation (birth certificate, membership card, etc.)		
	Other		
Additional requirements	Essay		
	Test scores (PSAT/NMSQT, SAT, etc.)		
	Other		
Recommendations needed?	Who/date requested		
	Date sent to program		
Submitting the application	Sign application/made copies		
	Pay application fee (amount), if needed		
	Applied online—received confirmation receipt		
	Applied by mail—confirm receipt of all materials		
Notification date(s)			
Send thank-you notes to everyone who helped.			

SCHOLARSHIP 3	SCHOLARSHIP 4	SCHOLARSHIP 5	SCHOLARSHIP 6

After the Letters Arrive

Next Steps After You're Accepted

Okay! You got into college. Take time to celebrate...but not too much. You still have to make some decisions and finalize some important things. Here's a list of what you'll need to take care of before you hit campus.

Read carefully what the college sent you

There's a reason why the envelope is fat. Much of the information will require prompt decisions and responses, so pay close attention to any deadlines.

Make a decision about financial aid

Your award letter will outline the various types of financial aid you've been offered, such as any scholarships, student loans, or work-study. Here are some tips to remember:

- If you've been accepted to more than one college, your final choice might depend upon which one offers the most aid. Use the "Compare Your Awards Worksheet" on page 182 to make sure you get it right.

- You're not required to accept the entire aid package as offered. The "Questions to Ask About Your Financial Aid Award" on page 183 will help you figure out what you should do.

- If there are any significant changes to your family's financial status or contact information, let the financial aid office know right away.

- Once you've made your decision, make sure you complete, sign, and return the form by the deadline.

Send the tuition deposit in on time

This is really important, because missing the date might cause you to lose your spot. Most colleges give you until May 1 to do this, but there are exceptions, so take note of the reply date in your acceptance letter. If you're up against the deadline, see if you can make the deposit online. If you're late, call the college right away.

Take care of loan paperwork

If you accept student loans as part of your financial aid package, you will need to fill out loan application forms before the start of the semester. You'll probably be required to take a loan counseling session online to make sure you understand your rights and obligations as a borrower.

Choose housing

If you're going to live on campus, at some point you'll receive a housing packet. This will include information about the dorms, a deposit form, move-in dates and instructions, roommate questionnaire, resident rules, and everything else you'll need to know. See "Choose Your Housing Options" on page 201 for more tips.

Contact your roommate

It's a good idea to get in touch and talk about who will bring things that will be shared, like a refrigerator or television. It will also make it easier to break the ice when you meet.

Select a meal plan

Most colleges offer a choice of different meal plans, typically based on how many meals per week you'll eat on campus. You may need to pick one before you get there, so think about your lifestyle—are you ever going to make it to breakfast?

Go shopping

Best advice—do it early. Check out the "Off-to-College Checklist" on page 204.

If you need a computer

There might be enough computers available on campus so you don't need to bring one, but that's rare. Even if you have a computer, you might need certain programs for the major you choose. It's a good idea to ask an adviser at the college about what you'll need.

Send your final grades

Confirm with your counselor that your final high school transcript will be mailed to your college's admission office.

Schedule a physical

Most colleges require that you submit the results of a recent physical exam, along with a vaccination history. You might also have to provide proof of health insurance. Try to take care of this paperwork before you arrive—otherwise you might not be able to register for classes.

Consider attending preorientation programs

Some colleges offer preorientation programs, where you take part in outdoor trips or urban community service projects. These programs are a great way to get to know people and get acclimated before school starts.

Prepare for placement exams

There's a good chance that you'll need to take one or more exams to determine your placement in science, math, writing, or language classes, so keep your brain from atrophying over the summer. Your previous standardized test scores could exempt you from certain placement exams, so find out the testing requirements and the exam schedule.

Thank those who helped you

Don't forget to express your gratitude to everyone who helped you during the college application process—counselors, teachers, coaches, scholarship sponsors, and especially your parents.

Sample Thanks, But No Thanks Letter

If more than one college accepted you, be sure to let the ones you won't attend know that you are declining their offer. That way, they can give your place to another candidate. It's also a courtesy that will hold you in good stead if you should ever decide to transfer to that school in the future.

Here's a quick-and-easy "thanks, but no thanks" sample letter.

> Your Name
> Street Address
> City, State, Zip
>
> April _ _, 20_ _
>
> Admission Office
> College/University
> Address
> City, State, Zip
>
> Dear [name of person on your acceptance letter]:
>
> I am writing to let you know that I must decline your offer of acceptance. I have decided to attend [name of college you are going to] instead.
>
> Thank you for accepting me. I consider it an honor.
>
> Sincerely,

What to Do If You're Wait-Listed

Being put on the wait-list by your first-choice school can be worse than being rejected—it hangs you up. If a college tells you that's where you are, try to decide whether you *really* want to attend that school before you agree to remain on the list.

But it doesn't have to be a passive waiting game. Here are some things you can do.

Get a better sense of your chances of admission

Colleges sometimes rank waiting lists. The higher you rank on the list the better your chances of being accepted. Contact the admission office to find out if it ranks wait-listed students or if it has a priority list. Most admission officers will tell you what you need to know.

Write a letter to the admission office

Being wait-listed means the school has already determined you have the academic credentials; so it's the nonacademic factors that count most now. Tell them about any achievements or new information that didn't make it onto your application. Emphasize your strong desire to attend the college and make a case for why you're a good fit. You can also enlist the help of an alumnus and your high school counselor.

Request another (or a first) interview

An interview can give you a personal contact— someone who can check on the status of your application.

Finish high school strong

This is no time to slack off. If you're wait-listed, you may be reevaluated based on your third- and fourth-quarter grades.

Stay involved

Show admission officers you're committed to sports, clubs, and other activities.

In the meantime, protect yourself

Look, chances of being accepted off of a wait list are never very good, and you won't find out if you've made it in or not until after the May 1 deadline to accept admission elsewhere has passed. So:

Reconsider the colleges that have accepted you

Your next-best choice isn't a bad choice— otherwise you wouldn't have applied there. Send in that deposit and plan to attend. You'll be surprised how much better you feel knowing that you have secured a place at a college that really wants you.

If you do get in, make sure it's still a good deal

Pay close attention to the conditions attached to being wait-listed; you may lose priority housing or financial aid options. Be sure to carefully compare the financial aid awards before you decide to forfeit your deposit and place at the other college.

Realize that you've already achieved something

Don't beat yourself up. You were wait-listed, not turned away. Many students were not as successful.

What to Do If You Don't Get in Anywhere

It happens—especially if students apply only to very selective schools or too few schools, or if senior year grades falter. You'll have to do some scrambling, but it's certainly not the end of the world. Here are some steps you can take.

Talk to your counselor

She or he has been through this before with other students and knows what to do.

Ask the colleges for an explanation

Was it your high school transcript? Your essay? Finding out will help you take stock and assess your options.

Apply to schools whose deadlines haven't yet passed

About half of all colleges have either no deadline or rolling admission. Use the College Search program on collegeboard.org to find schools that are still accepting applications. You'll have to act fast, but don't jump at a school just to have a place to go in September. It's hard to succeed at a school where you're not happy.

Consider transferring later

If you spend a year at another school, you can prove to college admission officers that you're motivated and ready for college-level work. You might want to think about a community college as a good, low-cost place to accomplish that.

Long shot: reapply or appeal

If their deadlines are open, some schools will let you reapply, which might make sense if you take the SAT again (it's offered in June) and improve your scores, or if your final senior-year grades shot up dramatically. If the deadline has passed, you can try to appeal your rejection. Most students don't win, but some colleges will allow you to provide new academic information, such as updated grades.

Consider spending a year doing something else worthwhile

Lots of students choose to take a "time-out" year between high school and college in order to do something they've always wanted to. Volunteering for a cause you really believe in, experimenting with different apprenticeships, or traveling to a place you've always dreamed of are experiences that can boost your college readiness and make you a more attractive applicant.

The upside

There's an upside? Yes. Sometimes a closed door points you to a better path. Maybe being forced to reevaluate your college choices will bring you to a better understanding of yourself, and what you really want. That will lead to better college choices and a better future—even if slightly delayed.

Remember, there's no one perfect college. Any number of schools can be good fits and make you happy. You'll get there.

Choose Your Housing Options

You may be offered a choice among different types of residence halls or room combinations. Every school has different housing options, but here are some of the most common.

Single-sex dorms

Some colleges require all first-year students to live in a single-sex dorm. Upside: You can let your hair down. Downside: There may be restrictions concerning guests of the opposite sex.

Substance-free dorms

Simple: no smoking, drinking, or drugs. Upside: You don't have to worry about your roommate throwing an all-night beer blast during finals. Downside: The penalties for getting caught with alcohol or drugs in these dorms can be harsh.

Special-interest or "theme" housing

In these dorms, you'll meet students who share your interests. For example, there may be a dorm for international students or music majors. Upside: You're more likely to make friends with kids taking the same classes as you. Downside: You may miss out on meeting a more diverse group of people.

> Most suites include a bathroom, but you and your suitemates will have to share the job of cleaning it.

Honors housing

These dorms are for students who want to learn where they live as well as in class. Involvement in special projects or community activities are encouraged, if not required; and designated "quiet times" for study are common. Upside: a richer college experience with less distractions during the week. Downside: You might not fit in if you find a structured environment too confining.

Different room options

Most residence halls consist of either double (or triple) rooms along a hallway, or suites with one or more bedrooms and a living room.

Singles. It's pretty rare to get a single room as a first-year student. Having a single has its obvious perks, but a roommate can be a welcome companion, especially those first few weeks. You may also find yourself being left alone when you don't want to be.

Doubles. That's you and a roommate in one room. It's by far the most common setup at most colleges. You usually get a desk, a lamp, a bureau, and a closet.

Suites. This is a nice option if you can get it. Suites usually consist of a couple of bedrooms and some kind of shared living space. For instance, a quad (four people) might be made up of two double bedrooms and one common room and one bathroom.

Thinking of Living Off Campus?

Getting an off-campus apartment (if your college allows it) may look like a more attractive option than the freshman dorms. But before you sign a lease, consider these pros, cons, and tips.

Pros

- Living off campus can be cheaper than on-campus housing, if you share the rent with one or more roommates, cook your own meals, and sublet over the summer.
- You'll probably have more independence, freedom, privacy, and space.
- Private apartments are usually quieter and have fewer distractions, and therefore (theoretically) are better for studying.
- Establishing a good rental history will make it easier to get a place after you graduate.
- You can eat on your own schedule, not the cafeteria's.
- You won't have to deal with communal bathrooms.

Cons

- You might miss out on many rich experiences available on campus. For freshmen living away, this is probably the most important factor to consider.
- If it's too far to walk to campus you'll also have the bother and expense of commuting.
- Dorms often offer fast, free Internet access and cable TV. You'll be on your own for those.
- You'll have to make time for chores: grocery shopping, preparing meals, cleaning.
- You may be mature enough to live completely on your own, but your roommates might not be. Nevertheless, you'll be committed to living with them for the rest of the year.

Think about what's important to you and put together your own list of pros and cons. You might also want to do a side-by-side comparison of all of the expenses involved. But if you've made up your mind to find an apartment (or have no other choice), here are some tips:

Where to find listings

- Your College's Off-Campus Housing Office: Many colleges have an off-campus housing office web page (or at least a bulletin board) where you can get housing, landlord, management company, and roommate listings. The office might also give you advice about topics such as: the best time to conduct your search, what to do if you encounter discrimination in your housing search, and how to resolve differences with your landlord or fellow tenants.
- Real Estate Agents: If you don't have the time to seek out and deal with landlords directly, a real estate agent can be a real convenience. Be aware that the fees can be considerable (a month's rent or more). Your college's off-campus housing office may have arrangements with local real estate agents for reduced fees for students.
- Search the Web: Many students have luck conducting their apartment hunt online, using Craig's List, Oodle, or other websites (e.g., apartments.com, ApartmentGuide.com) to find apartments near their college.
- Neighborhood Listings: Check local newspapers, bulletin boards, and apartment guides.

Search tips

Expect plenty of competition for choice apartments before the semester begins. The better prepared you are, the better your chances of landing the apartment you want.

- Start your search as early as possible—up to four weeks before the start of the semester. While you're looking, consider staying with friends or family, or in a hotel or short-term residence.
- Be prepared to put a deposit down on the spot. (Make sure to get a receipt.)
- Most landlords renting to students require a parent or other adult to cosign the lease as guarantor. You and your guarantor should be ready to provide the following documentation: last year's tax return, recent pay stubs, personal and business references, contact information for previous landlords, and photo identification.

Signing a lease

A lease is a binding, legal contract between you and your landlord. It's essential that you and your parents read it carefully and understand and agree to everything before signing. Staff at your college's off-campus housing office may also be able to review your lease and give you advice.

Get it in writing

Don't be afraid to negotiate any part of the lease with your landlord. Remember, your landlord is only obligated to provide services explicitly stated in your lease and under the housing laws. So if you want it—get it in writing. Here are some additional lease tips to remember:

- Pay special attention to any riders attached to your lease, as these are just as binding as anything else in your lease.
- Make sure you understand the exact terms of renewing or terminating your lease, getting your security deposit back, and subletting your apartment.
- If you are renting with a group of people, is everyone named in the lease? Can each tenant sign separate leases?
- Do you understand what kinds of repairs your landlord is responsible for? Find out what types of improvements you are allowed to make.
- If you have questions about rent guidelines, maintenance codes, or your rights and responsibilities, contact the state attorney general's office or local chamber of commerce.

Off-to-College Checklist

Use this checklist to make sure you have everything you need for your first year at college. Each person's needs are different, so tailor this list to suit yourself.

Clothing Guidelines

- ☐ 12 pairs of underwear
- ☐ 12 pairs of socks (more if you play sports)
- ☐ 5 pairs of pants/jeans
- ☐ 12 shirts/blouses
- ☐ 2 sets of sweats
- ☐ Pajamas
- ☐ Slippers and/or flip-flops
- ☐ 2 sweaters (if it gets cold)
- ☐ Light/heavy jackets
- ☐ Waterproof hooded jacket or raincoat
- ☐ Gloves/scarf/hat (if it gets cold)
- ☐ 1 pair of boots
- ☐ 2 pairs of sneakers or comfortable/walking shoes
- ☐ 1 set of "business casual" attire (optional)

Kitchen Stuff

- ☐ Plastic bowl and cup
- ☐ Coffee mug
- ☐ Plastic forks, knives, spoons
- ☐ Can/bottle opener

Room Needs/Storage

- ☐ Bedside lamp
- ☐ Alarm clock/clock radio
- ☐ Wastepaper basket
- ☐ Storage bins
- ☐ Under-the-bed storage trays
- ☐ Lots of hangers
- ☐ Desk lamp
- ☐ Fan
- ☐ Drying rack
- ☐ Bulletin board and push pins
- ☐ Dry erase wall calendar/board
- ☐ Toolkit

Electronics

- ☐ Laptop computer and printer
- ☐ Ethernet cord, modem, router
- ☐ Surge protector
- ☐ Extension cords
- ☐ 3 two-prong adapters
- ☐ Portable music player
- ☐ Headphones
- ☐ Adapter/charger(s)

Linens/Laundry Supplies

- ☐ Sheets and pillowcases (2 sets. Check with school for size needed—some college twin beds are extra long.)
- ☐ Towels (3 each of bath, hand, and face)
- ☐ Pillows (2)
- ☐ Mattress pad (Check with school for size needed.)
- ☐ Blankets (2)
- ☐ Comforter/bed spread
- ☐ Clothes hangers
- ☐ Laundry bag/basket
- ☐ Laundry marking pen
- ☐ Laundry stain remover
- ☐ Roll(s) of quarters
- ☐ Lint brush
- ☐ Sewing kit

Toiletries/Misc.

- Antacid
- Aspirin or other pain relievers
- Vitamins
- Antidiarrheal medicine
- Adhesive bandages
- Cough drops
- Shower tote
- Shampoo and conditioner
- Hair-styling products
- Bath and face soap
- Traveling-soap container(s)
- Toothpaste and toothbrush
- Dental floss
- Comb/brush
- Tweezers
- Nail clippers
- Hair dryer
- Razor and shaving cream
- Lotion and/or facial moisturizer
- Cotton swabs
- Umbrella
- Backpack
- Camera

Office/Desk Supplies

- Memory sticks
- Phone/address book
- Stapler and staples
- Printer paper
- Pens and pencils
- Pencil holder and sharpener
- Notebooks
- 3 x 5 cards
- Post-it notes
- Paper clips
- Rubber bands
- Scissors
- Highlighter pens (multiple colors)
- Ruler
- Stackable desk trays (at least 4)
- Dictionary
- Thesaurus
- Stamps/envelopes

Shared Items —Check with roommate(s)

- Audio equipment
- TV and DVD player
- Coffeemaker/hot pot
- Microwave/toaster oven
- Small refrigerator
- Area rug
- Posters/art

These Can Be Purchased Upon Arrival

- Paper towels
- Trash bags
- Lightbulbs
- All-purpose cleaner
- Plastic storage bags
- Food storage containers
- Laundry detergent
- Fabric softener
- Dish soap
- Wet wipes
- Tissues

Shopping and Packing Tips

Does shopping and packing to go away to college sound like fun…or agony? Either way, the best advice is: start early.

Be a savvy shopper

Make a budget and stick to it—and keep in mind that not everything you take to college needs to be new.

What do you have? What do you need?

Before you start shopping, make an honest appraisal of what you have. Separate out the nice-to-haves from the must-haves—if you still want them, you can retrieve them during a homecoming break. If you've still got more than you can manage during your trip, separate out some nonessentials and arrange to have them shipped to you after your arrival.

Getting your stuff to the dorm

If you're flying to school, not driving, you'll need to think about how to get all of your stuff there. You can shop at home, and ship all of the things you will need to school. Or, you can do your shopping once you get there, provided you have a way of getting all your things back to the dorm.

The easiest option might be to do all your shopping online and have it all shipped to you at school (shipping might even be free). And remember: you don't have to bring everything all at once, unless you plan to never go home anytime during the year.

More packing advice

Here are a few more tips to help you with your planning:

- Start early—it minimizes stress and promotes family harmony. You don't want to spend your last few days at home arguing with Mom and Dad about what you're planning to take with you.

- Don't forget the things that will make your dorm room feel like home—photographs of family and friends, important mementos, or anything else that will make your new room your own space.

- Don't bring a full four-season wardrobe. Remember that most dorm-room closets are fairly small. You'll be able to retrieve extra stuff from home during breaks.

- Don't overestimate how often you'll be doing laundry. It will probably be weeks, not days, between loads—so bring as many socks and undies as you possibly can.

- Know thyself. If you never iron and your idea of getting dressed up is changing from torn jeans to khakis, then don't waste precious closet space with an ironing board you won't use or dress clothes you won't wear.

- Check with roommates to avoid duplication—space is tight (so are electric outlets, generally) so divvy up the large items.

- Duffle bags are great—they can be stored under a mattress when not in use. (Just don't forget they're there!) Plastic storage bins (you can get them at most grocery stores) are good too, and usually fit under the bed.

College
Survival Tips

No matter if you live home or go away, college is going to be a lot different from high school. Big changes can be stressful at first, but the more you know about what's coming, the easier it will be to handle it. Here are some realities, and a few commonsense ways to deal with them.

The work is harder and there's more of it

Courses are at a higher level than high school classes and the material is presented at a faster pace. Plus, professors are likely to assign more reading, writing, and problem sets than you may be used to.

...Your strategy:

Not to panic. Realize that all freshmen struggle with the work load at first, but it smooths out after a while. Study groups help a lot. And while you'll have more work, you'll also have more free time than you did in high school— enough to get the work done and have fun too. Most important: Kick the procrastination habit. It's much easier to keep up than to catch up.

Nobody will be looking over your shoulder

Here's a downside to being treated like an adult: Professors will tell you at the beginning of the semester what the course requirements are, and expect you to turn in the work on time without any reminders. If you cut classes and don't do assignments, no one will nag you.

...Your strategy:

Use a calendar to keep track of when and where your classes meet, when assignments are due, and when tests will take place. If you miss a class, be sure to get the notes from someone— the material won't be covered again. If you're used to being kept on track by a nag, nag yourself with sticky notes.

More independence—and responsibility

You won't have the same day-to-day support system you may have had at home. For example, how will you manage your money so you don't go broke midsemester, or into credit card debt? Who will make sure you're not getting sick or run down?

...Your strategy:

Make smart decisions. For example, when it comes to your money, stick to a budget and use credit cards only for real emergencies. When it comes to your health, try to avoid all-nighters or skipping meals, and pay attention to what your body tells you.

A new social scene

You'll be thrown into new experiences and face lots of choices. Suddenly, you can recreate yourself in any way you want. But while you will be meeting many new people, you might feel lonely in a crowd at first.

...Your strategy:

Remember that true friendships are formed slowly. A good way to find kindred spirits is to openly pursue your own interests—most campuses offer "student life" opportunities to do that. If you are facing challenges and need someone to talk to, reach out. If you live in a dorm, talk to the RA (resident assistant). In college, it's up to you to find help, but there is a lot of help available: teachers, counselors, support services, and campus ministers. You won't be alone.

Glossary

Glossary

Definitions of commonly used terms vary from college to college. Consult specific college catalogs or their websites for more detailed information.

Academic adviser. A professor assigned to help students choose appropriate courses each semester. Many students consult their adviser for help in selecting a major.

Accreditation. Recognition by an accrediting organization or agency that a college meets acceptable standards in its programs, facilities, and services. National or regional accreditation applies to a college as a whole and not to any particular programs or courses of study. Some programs within colleges, such as the engineering or nursing program, may be accredited by professional organizations.

ACT. A college entrance examination given at test centers in the United States and other countries on specified dates. Please visit the organization's website for further information.

Adjunct professor. A member of the faculty who is not on the track for tenure and may teach part time or full time. Some colleges may refer to adjuncts as "lecturers" or "visiting professors."

AP (Advanced Placement Program). An academic program of the College Board that provides high school students with the opportunity to study and learn at the college level. Most colleges and universities in the United States accept qualifying AP Exam scores for credit, advanced placement, or both.

Articulation agreement. A formal agreement between two higher educational institutions (usually two- and four-year colleges), regarding recognition and acceptance of course credits, and designed to make it easy for students to transfer without duplication of course work.

Associate degree. A degree granted by a college or university after the satisfactory completion of the equivalent of a two-year, full-time program of study.

Award letter. A means of notifying admitted students of the financial aid the college is offering them. The award letter provides information on the types and amounts of aid offered, the conditions that govern the awards, and a deadline for accepting the awards.

Bachelor's, or baccalaureate, degree. A degree received after the satisfactory completion of a four- or five-year, full-time program of study (or its part-time equivalent) at a college or university. The bachelor of arts (B.A.), bachelor of science (B.S.), and bachelor of fine arts (B.F.A.) are the most common bachelor's degrees. Policies concerning their award vary from college to college.

Branch campus. A campus that is affiliated with another college. Branch campuses may not have the full array of majors and services offered by the main campus.

Bursar. The college official responsible for handling billing and payments for tuition, fees, housing, etc.

Candidates' reply date. The date by which admitted students must accept or decline an offer of admission and (if any) the college's offer of financial aid. Most colleges and universities do not require a decision from accepted applicants for the fall semester before May 1. That way applicants have time to hear from all the colleges to which they have applied before having to make a commitment to any of them.

Academic unit. A unit of credit given for successful completion of one year's study of a college-preparatory or academic subject in high school.

Career college. Usually a for-profit two-year college that trains students for specific occupations. Also known as a vocational/technical school.

CB code. A four-digit College Board code number that students use to designate colleges or scholarship programs to receive their SAT score reports.

Certificate. An award for completing a particular program or course of study, usually given by two-year colleges or vocational/technical schools for non-degree programs of a year or less.

CLEP (College-Level Examination Program). A program in which students receive college credit by earning a qualifying score in any of 33 examinations in business, composition and literature, world languages, history and social sciences, and science and mathematics. Sponsored by the College Board, CLEP exams are administered at over 1,700 test centers. Over 2,900 colleges and universities grant credit for passing a CLEP exam.

College. The generic term for an institution of higher learning (after high school) leading to an associate or bachelor's degree; also a term used to designate divisions within a university (such as the college of engineering or the college of liberal arts).

College-preparatory subjects. Areas of high school study required for admission to, or recommended as preparation for, college. College-prep subjects usually include English, history and social studies, foreign languages, mathematics, science, and the arts.

Common application. The standard application form used by colleges who are subscribers to the Common Application Group. Applicants need to fill out the form only once, and can then submit it to any number of the participating colleges.

Community/junior college. A two-year college. Community colleges are public, whereas junior colleges are private. Both usually offer vocational programs as well as the first two years of a four-year program.

Concentration. A specialized branch of study within a major. For example, students majoring in history might choose to concentrate on the Renaissance; in fulfilling the requirements of the major, they would select several courses focusing on that time period.

Conditional acceptance. Admission offered on the condition that the student successfully complete specified requirements such as attending summer school, taking remedial courses, or maintaining a certain GPA during the first semester of study.

Consortium. A group of colleges that offer services and learning opportunities to the students of any college within the consortium. The consortium may share libraries, athletic resources, extracurricular activities, faculty, and more.

Cooperative education (co-op). A career-oriented program in which students alternate between class attendance and related employment in business, industry, or government. The employment stints are typically arranged by the program, and students usually receive both academic credit and payment for their work. Under a cooperative plan, a bachelor's degree usually takes an extra year to complete, but graduates have the advantage of about a year's practical work experience in addition to their studies.

Core curriculum. A group of courses, in varied areas of the arts and sciences, designated by a college as one of the requirements for a degree. See also *general education requirements.*

Cost of attendance. A number of expenses including tuition and fees (including loan fees), books and supplies, and student's living expenses while attending school. The cost of attendance is compared with the student's expected family contribution to determine the student's need for financial aid.

Credit hour. A standard unit of measurement for a college course. Each credit hour represents one classroom hour per week. Credit hours are used to determine the total number of hours needed to complete the requirements of a degree, diploma, certificate, or other formal award.

Credit/placement by examination. Academic credit or placement out of introductory courses granted by a college to entering students who have demonstrated proficiency in college-level studies through examinations such as those sponsored by the College Board's AP and CLEP programs.

Cross-registration. The practice of permitting students enrolled at one college or university to enroll in courses at another institution without formally applying for admission to the second institution.

CSS Profile. An application and service offered by the College Board and used by some colleges, universities, and private scholarship programs to award their own private financial aid funds.

Deferred admission. The practice of permitting students to postpone enrollment, usually for one year, after acceptance to the college.

Degree. An award given by a college or university certifying that a student has completed a course of study. See also *certificate.*

Department: A unit within a college consisting of all faculty in a certain discipline, and including related programs of study. The Romance languages department, for example, may include programs in French, Italian, and Spanish.

Discipline. An academic area of study. Literature, history, social science, natural science, mathematics, the arts, and foreign language are disciplines; each takes a certain approach to knowledge.

Distance learning. An option for earning course credit off-campus via the Internet, satellite classes, videotapes, correspondence courses, or other means. See also *virtual university.*

Doctoral degree (doctorate). See *graduate degree.*

Dormitory. See *residence hall.*

Double major. Any program in which a student completes the requirements of two majors at the same time.

Dual enrollment. The practice of students enrolling in college courses while still in high school.

Early Action. A nonbinding application program in which a student can receive an early admission decision from one or more colleges but is not required to accept the admission offer or to make a deposit before May 1. Compare to *early decision*, which is a binding program.

Early Action single choice. An Early Action program in which the student may only apply Early Action to one college or university.

Early Decision. Students who apply under Early Decision make a commitment to enroll at the college if admitted and offered a satisfactory financial aid package. Application deadlines are usually in November or December with a mid-to-late December notification date. Some colleges have two rounds of Early Decision.

EFC (Expected family contribution). The total amount students and their families are expected to pay toward college costs from their income and assets for one academic year.

Elective. A course that is not required for one's chosen major or the college's core curriculum, and can be used to fulfill the credit hour requirement for graduation.

Exchange student program. Any arrangement that permits a student to study for a semester or more at another college in the United States without extending the amount of time required for a degree.

FAFSA (Free Application for Federal Student Aid). A form completed by all applicants for federal student aid. Most colleges require the FAFSA for awarding their own institutional funds, and in many states, completion of the FAFSA is also sufficient to establish eligibility for state-sponsored aid programs.

Federal code number. A six-digit number that identifies a specific college to which students want their FAFSA form submitted. Also known as Title IV number.

Federal Direct Loan Program. An education loan program in which students and parents borrow directly from the U.S. Department of Education instead of a commercial bank. Direct loans include the Stafford Loan, PLUS loan, and Loan Consolidation programs.

Financial aid package. What a college offers to an accepted student who has applied for aid; usually a mix of grants, loans, and/or work-study. See also *award letter*.

Financial need. The difference between a student's expected family contribution (EFC) and the cost of attending a particular college.

For-profit college. A private institution operated by its owners as a profit-making enterprise. (Most private colleges are nonprofit.) Also known as a proprietary college.

4-1-4 calendar. A variation of the semester calendar system, the 4-1-4 calendar consists of two terms of about 16 weeks each, separated by a one-month intersession used for intensive short courses, independent study, off-campus work, or other types of instruction.

General education requirements. Courses that give undergraduates background in the primary academic disciplines: natural sciences, social sciences, mathematics, literature and language, and fine arts. Most colleges require students to take general education courses in their first and second years, as a way to sample a wide range of courses before choosing a major. At some colleges, general education courses are referred to as the core curriculum; at others, a few courses within the general education requirements are core courses that all students must take.

Grade point average (GPA) or ratio. A system used by many schools for evaluating the overall scholastic performance of students. Grade points are determined by first multiplying the number of hours given for a course by the numerical value of the grade and then dividing the sum of all grade points by the total number of hours carried. The most common system of numerical values for grades is $A = 4$, $B = 3$, $C = 2$, $D = 1$, and E or $F = 0$.

Graduate degree. A degree pursued after a student has earned a bachelor's degree. The master's degree, which requires one to three years of study, is usually the degree earned after the bachelor's. The doctoral degree requires further study.

Greek life. The fraternity and sorority community at a college. Joining a Greek society (so called because each is named with letters of the Greek alphabet) is optional. Greek organizations have different missions and themes; some are service oriented. Greek life can be a large or small part of a campus.

Hispanic-serving college. A college where Hispanic students comprise at least 25 percent of the full-time undergraduate enrollment.

Historically black college. An institution founded prior to 1964 whose mission was historically, and remains, the education of African Americans.

Honors program. Any special program for very able students that offers the opportunity for educational enrichment, independent study, acceleration, or some combination of these.

Humanities. The branches of learning that usually include art, the classics, dramatic art, English, general and comparative literature, journalism, music, philosophy, and religion. Many colleges divide their offerings into three divisions: humanities, social sciences, and natural sciences.

Independent study. Academic work chosen or designed by the student with the approval of the department concerned, under an instructor's supervision. This work is usually undertaken outside of the regular classroom structure.

In-district tuition. The tuition charged by a community college or state university to residents of the district from which it draws tax support. Districts are usually individual counties or cities, but sometimes are larger.

In-state tuition. The tuition that a public institution charges residents of its state. Some community colleges and state universities charge this rate to students who are not residents of their district, but who are residents of their state.

International Baccalaureate (IB). A high school curriculum offered by some schools in the United States and other countries. Some colleges award credit for completion of this curriculum. Please visit the organization's website for further information.

Internship. A short-term, supervised work experience, usually related to a student's major field, for which the student earns academic credit. The work can be full- or part-time, on- or off-campus, paid or unpaid.

Intersession term. A short term offered between semesters. See also *4-1-4 calendar*.

Junior college. See *community/junior college*.

Liberal arts. The study of the humanities (literature, the arts, and philosophy), history, foreign languages, social sciences, mathematics, and natural sciences. The focus is on the development of general knowledge and reasoning ability rather than specific skills.

Liberal arts college. A college where study is focused on the liberal arts, with little emphasis on pre-professional training. Most liberal arts colleges are privately controlled. They generally don't offer as many majors in the technical or scientific disciplines as comprehensive colleges or universities.

Lower-division courses. Courses that students are expected to take in their first two years of college. These courses lay the foundation for further study in the subject area.

Major. The field of study in which students concentrate, or specialize, during their undergraduate study. See also *concentration* and *minor*.

Master's degree. See *graduate degree*.

Merit aid. Financial aid awarded on the basis of academic achievement, artistic or athletic talent, leadership qualities, or similar traits. Financial need may or may not be an additional requirement.

Minor. Course work that is not as extensive as that in a major but gives students some specialized knowledge of a second field.

Need-based financial aid. Financial aid (scholarships, grants, loans, or work-study opportunities) awarded on the basis of a family's inability to pay the full cost of attending a particular college.

Open admission. The college admission policy of admitting high school graduates and other adults generally without regard to conventional academic qualifications, such as high school subjects, high school grades, and admission test scores. Virtually all applicants with high school diplomas or their equivalent are accepted, space permitting.

Out-of-state tuition. The tuition a public college or university charges residents of other states. Out-of-state tuition can be three to four times as much as the in-state rate.

Pell Grant. A federally sponsored and administered need-based grant to undergraduate students. Congress annually sets the dollar range. Eligibility is based on a student's expected family contribution, the total cost of attendance at the college, and whether the student is attending the college full time or part time.

Perkins loan. A low-interest, federally funded campus-based loan, based on need, for undergraduate study. Repayment is deferred until completion of the student's education, and may be further deferred for limited periods of service in the military, Peace Corps, or approved comparable organizations. The total debt may be forgiven by the federal government if the recipient enters a career of service as a public health nurse, law enforcement officer, public school teacher, or social worker.

Placement test. A battery of tests designed to assess a student's aptitude and level of achievement in various academic areas so that he or she can select the most appropriate courses.

PLUS loan (Parent's Loan for Undergraduate Students). A federal direct loan program that permits parents of undergraduate students to borrow up to the full cost of education, less any other financial aid the student may have received.

Portfolio. A collection of examples of a student's work assembled to provide a representation of the student's achievements and skill level.

Preprofessional program. An advising program and recommended course of study for undergraduate students intending to pursue a professional degree after college. Although there is no prescribed major for entrance to professional school, students planning for a career in law, ministry, or a medical profession need to take an undergraduate program that lays the groundwork for their training.

Premed students, for example, must complete certain science courses. Preprofessional advisers help students plan their undergraduate studies and to prepare for admission to professional school.

Priority date. The date by which an application, whether for admission, housing, or financial aid, must be received in order to be given the strongest consideration. After that date, qualified applicants are considered on a first-come, first-served basis, and only for as long as slots and/or funds are available.

Private college/university. An institution of higher education not supported by public funds. Private colleges may be not-for-profit or for-profit (proprietary), independent, or church-affiliated.

Provost. A senior academic administrator; typically the head of a college within a university.

PSAT/NMSQT (Preliminary SAT/National Merit Scholarship Qualifying Test). A comprehensive program that helps schools put students on the path to college. The PSAT/NMSQT is administered by high schools to sophomores and juniors each year in October and serves as the qualifying test for scholarships awarded by the National Merit Scholarship Corporation.

Public college/university. An institution that is supported by taxes and other public revenue and governed by a county, state, or federal government agency.

Quarter. An academic calendar period of about 12 weeks. Four quarters make up an academic year, but at colleges using the quarter system, students make normal progress by attending three quarters each year. In some colleges, students can accelerate their progress by attending all four quarters in one or more years.

Reach school. A college you'd like to attend, but will be difficult for you to get in. Your GPA and test scores may be below average for this school, but some other aspect of your application may make up for that. You should apply to one or two reach schools.

Registrar. The college official responsible for registering students for classes, and keeping academic records.

Regular admission. Admission during the college's normal calendar for admission, as opposed to Early Decision or Early Action admission.

Reciprocity agreement. An agreement between neighboring states that allows residents to attend a public college in either state at the in-state tuition rate.

Residence hall. An on-campus living facility. Also known as a dormitory (or "dorm").

Residency requirement. The minimum number of terms that a student must spend taking courses on campus (as opposed to independent study, transfer credits from other colleges, or credit-by-examination) to be eligible for graduation. Can also refer to the minimum amount of time a student must have lived in-state in order to qualify for the in-state tuition rate at a public college or university.

Returning adult. An entering college student who has been out of high school a year or more. Some colleges also have an age threshold.

Rolling admission. An admission procedure by which the college considers each student's application as soon as all the required credentials, such as school record and test scores, have been received. The college usually notifies an applicant of its decision without delay. At many colleges, rolling admission allows for early notification and works much like nonbinding Early Action programs.

Safety school. A college you'd like to attend that's also sure to accept you. Usually a public institution in your state that is not selective in its admission criteria or practices open admissions. You should apply to at least one safety school.

SAT. A college entrance exam that tests critical reading, writing, and mathematical skills, given on specified dates throughout the year at test centers in the United States and other countries. The SAT is used by most colleges and sponsors of financial aid programs.

SAT Subject Test. Admission tests in specific subjects, given at test centers in the United States and other countries on specified dates throughout the year. Used by colleges not only to help with decisions about admission but also in course placement and exemption of enrolled freshmen.

Self-help aid. Student financial aid, such as loans and jobs, that requires repayment or employment.

Semester. A term or period of about 16 weeks. Colleges on a semester system offer two periods of instruction, fall and spring, a year; there may also be a summer session (usually a shorter, more concentrated period of time).

Sophomore standing. Consideration of a as a sophomore for academic purposes such as registering for classes and declaring majors. A college may grant incoming freshmen sophomore standing if they have enough credits from AP, CLEP, or IB exams.

Stafford loan. A federal direct loan program that allows students to borrow money for educational expenses. Subsidized Stafford loans are offered by colleges based on need; the federal government pays the interest while the borrower is in college. Unsubsidized Stafford loans are non-need-based; the interest begins accumulating immediately. For both programs, repayment does not begin until after college, and the amounts that may be borrowed depend on the student's year in school.

Student Aid Report (SAR). A report produced by the U.S. Department of Education and sent to students in response to their having filed the Free Application for Federal Student Aid (FAFSA). The SAR contains information the student provided on the FAFSA as well as the resulting expected family contribution, which the financial aid office will use in determining the student's eligibility for a Federal Pell Grant and other federal student aid programs.

Study abroad. Any arrangement by which a student completes part of the college program—typically the junior year but sometimes only a semester or a summer—studying in another country. A college may operate a campus abroad, or it may have a cooperative agreement with some other U.S. college or an institution of the other country.

Subsidized loan. A loan awarded to a student on the basis of financial need. The federal government or the state awarding the loan pays the borrower's interest while they are in college at least half-time, thereby subsidizing the loan.

Teacher certification. A college program designed to prepare students to meet the requirements for certification as teachers in elementary and secondary schools.

Technical college. A college with an emphasis on education and training in technical fields.

Term. The shorter period into which colleges divide the school year. Some colleges are on the semester system, in which students complete two semesters, or terms, each year. Others are on the quarter system, in which they attend three quarters each year. Many colleges offer a summer term, so that students can attend college year-round and thus receive their degree more quickly, or can finish incomplete credits.

Terminal degree. The highest degree level attainable in a particular field. For most teaching faculty this is a doctoral degree. In certain fields, however, a master's degree is the highest level.

Transcript. A copy of a student's official academic record listing all courses taken and grades received.

Transfer program. An education program in a two-year college (or a four-year college that offers associate degrees), primarily for students who plan to continue their studies in a four-year college or university.

Trimester. An academic calendar period of about 15 weeks. Three trimesters make up one year. Students normally progress by attending two of the trimesters each year and in some colleges can accelerate their programs by attending all three trimesters in one or more years.

Tuition. The price of instruction at a college. Tuition may be charged per term or per credit hour.

Undergraduate. A student in the freshman, sophomore, junior, or senior year of study, as opposed to a graduate student who has earned an undergraduate degree and is pursuing a master's, doctoral, or professional degree.

University. An institution of higher education that is divided into several colleges, schools or institutes. Students typically have to apply for admission to a specific college, which may have its own requirements. Generally, university students take classes in the college to which they were accepted, but have access to shared facilities such as libraries and laboratories.

Upper division. The junior and senior years of study.

Upper-division college. A college offering bachelor's degree programs that begin with the junior year. Entering students must have completed their freshman and sophomore years at other colleges.

Virtual university. A degree-granting, accredited institution wherein all courses are delivered by distance learning, with no physical campus.

Wait-list. A list of students who meet the admission requirements, but will only be offered a place in the class if space becomes available.

Work-study. An arrangement by which a student combines employment and college study. The employment may be an integral part of the academic program (as in cooperative education and internships) or simply a means of paying for college (as in the Federal Work-Study Program).

Contacts

SCHOOL NAME_____

ADDRESS_____

CONTACT 1	CONTACT 2	CONTACT 3
NAME	NAME	NAME
TITLE	TITLE	TITLE
E-MAIL	E-MAIL	E-MAIL
PHONE/CELL	PHONE/CELL	PHONE/CELL
FAX	FAX	FAX
WHY IMPORTANT	WHY IMPORTANT	WHY IMPORTANT

SCHOOL NAME_____

ADDRESS_____

CONTACT 1	CONTACT 2	CONTACT 3
NAME	NAME	NAME
TITLE	TITLE	TITLE
E-MAIL	E-MAIL	E-MAIL
PHONE/CELL	PHONE/CELL	PHONE/CELL
FAX	FAX	FAX
WHY IMPORTANT	WHY IMPORTANT	WHY IMPORTANT

SCHOOL NAME _____

ADDRESS _____

CONTACT 1	CONTACT 2	CONTACT 3
NAME	NAME	NAME
TITLE	TITLE	TITLE
E-MAIL	E-MAIL	E-MAIL
PHONE/CELL	PHONE/CELL	PHONE/CELL
FAX	FAX	FAX
WHY IMPORTANT	WHY IMPORTANT	WHY IMPORTANT

SCHOOL NAME _____

ADDRESS _____

CONTACT 1	CONTACT 2	CONTACT 3
NAME	NAME	NAME
TITLE	TITLE	TITLE
E-MAIL	E-MAIL	E-MAIL
PHONE/CELL	PHONE/CELL	PHONE/CELL
FAX	FAX	FAX
WHY IMPORTANT	WHY IMPORTANT	WHY IMPORTANT

SCHOOL NAME _____

ADDRESS _____

CONTACT 1	CONTACT 2	CONTACT 3
NAME	NAME	NAME
TITLE	TITLE	TITLE
E-MAIL	E-MAIL	E-MAIL
PHONE/CELL	PHONE/CELL	PHONE/CELL
FAX	FAX	FAX
WHY IMPORTANT	WHY IMPORTANT	WHY IMPORTANT

SCHOOL NAME _____

ADDRESS _____

CONTACT 1	CONTACT 2	CONTACT 3
NAME	NAME	NAME
TITLE	TITLE	TITLE
E-MAIL	E-MAIL	E-MAIL
PHONE/CELL	PHONE/CELL	PHONE/CELL
FAX	FAX	FAX
WHY IMPORTANT	WHY IMPORTANT	WHY IMPORTANT

SCHOOL NAME _____

ADDRESS _____

CONTACT 1	CONTACT 2	CONTACT 3
NAME	NAME	NAME
TITLE	TITLE	TITLE
E-MAIL	E-MAIL	E-MAIL
PHONE/CELL	PHONE/CELL	PHONE/CELL
FAX	FAX	FAX
WHY IMPORTANT	WHY IMPORTANT	WHY IMPORTANT

SCHOOL NAME _____

ADDRESS _____

CONTACT 1	CONTACT 2	CONTACT 3
NAME	NAME	NAME
TITLE	TITLE	TITLE
E-MAIL	E-MAIL	E-MAIL
PHONE/CELL	PHONE/CELL	PHONE/CELL
FAX	FAX	FAX
WHY IMPORTANT	WHY IMPORTANT	WHY IMPORTANT